CHINESE MASSAGE

FOR INFANTS AND CHILDREN

CHINESE MASSAGE

FOR INFANTS AND CHILDREN

Traditional Techniques

for Alleviating

Colic, Colds, Earaches, and

Other Common Childhood Conditions

Kyle Cline

Healing Arts Press
Rochester, Vermont

Healing Arts Press
One Park Street
Rochester, Vermont 05767
www.InnerTraditions.com

Healing Arts Press is a division of Inner Traditions International

*Note to the reader: This book is intended as an informational guide. The remedies, approaches, and techniques described
herein are meant to supplement, and not to be a substitute for, professional medical care or treatment.
They should not be used to treat a serious ailment without prior consultation with a qualified health care professional.*

LIBRARY OF CONGRESS CATALOGING-IN-PUBLICATION DATA
Cline, Kyle, 1957–
Chinese massage for infants and children : techniques for alleviating colic, colds, earaches,
and other common childhood conditions / Kyle Cline.
p. cm.
Includes bibliographical references and index.
ISBN 0-89281-797-6 (alk. paper)
1. Massage for infants. 2. Medicine, Chinese. 3. Massage for children. I. Title.
RJ53.M35C57   1999
615.8'22'0830951—dc21   99-18421
CIP

Printed and bound in Canada

10   9   8   7   6   5   4   3   2   1

Text design and layout by Virginia L. Scott
This book was typeset in Goudy with Lucida Sans as the display typeface
Graphic illustrations: Sheila Lucas
Photograph credits: Jeanne Ellis and Rita Smith

CONTENTS

ACKNOWLEDGMENTS

ANY BOOK OF THIS SCOPE IS THE FINAL PRODUCT OF MANY people's efforts. While I take responsibility for any errors, credit is due to many more people than would fit on this page.

I wish to acknowledge the many generations of doctors in China whose efforts have culminated in the current practice of Chinese pediatric massage. I would also like to acknowledge the generous help and support of my teachers and friends: Dr. Huang Da-gang, Dr. Li Hong-wai, Dr. Zheng Shou-jie, Dr. Shen Yang-he, Dr. Lin, Dr. Ye, Dr. Ting Ji-feng, Wu Jun-miao, Nurse Lu, Ye Jing, and Antoine Eid.

I acknowledge the invaluable help of my teachers, colleagues, and friends in the United States: Bob Flaws, Honora Wolfe, Master Mantak Chia, Maneewan Chia, Subhuti Dharmananda, Dr. Edythe Vickers, Dr. Zhang Qing-cai, Judith Rose, Peggy Nauman, Sheila Lucas, Karen Sprute-Francovich, Aaron Norr, and Helaine Gross.

I greatly appreciate the support and assistance provided by the staff of Healing Arts Press, especially Peri Champine, Susan Davidson, Jon Graham, Blake Maher, and Virginia Scott, and copy editor Laura Jorstad.

Finally, my deepest appreciation to the many children and parents, both Chinese and American, who have contributed to my understanding of Chinese pediatric massage.

PREFACE

TODAY MANY ADULTS ARE EXPLORING A WIDE ARRAY of alternatives to the Western (allopathic) style of health care. Allopathic medicine offers many useful services but does not deal well with all conditions. This is as true for children as it is for adults. Unfortunately, there are few alternative medical models available for children's health care in the United States.

This book describes a very sophisticated pediatric massage system that has been used in China for over one thousand years. It is not well known in the United States at this time, but that is changing. Throughout its long history in China, pediatric massage has proven to be a viable option for treating a wide variety of common childhood conditions.

This book was first developed to educate the parents of the children I was treating in my practice. Many parents were interested in learning how to give massage at home to supplement my treatments. Other parents wanted to know what they could do for simple conditions that did not require a professional massage.

The result is this reference book with which parents can learn how to use Chinese massage for their own children. You may use it to learn one or two points to ease a condition or to learn how to give a complete massage.

In simple cases the information in this book may be sufficient for home massage. In more difficult conditions massage may be one part of an overall treatment strategy that includes other types of medical care.

Another purpose of this book is to demystify the sometimes difficult concepts of Chinese medicine so that you as a parent can understand and use this information to benefit your children.

Pediatric massage is a specialty within the professional field of Chinese medicine.

However, a degree in Chinese medicine or massage is not required to use this technique for simple conditions. The requirements to learn and perform pediatric massage well are:

- An open mind
- The intention to do well
- A willingness to try something new
- Staying within the limits of your abilities

At a time when many people are rethinking what kind of health care best suits their needs, looking to different medical models can provide a new perspective. The rapid growth and general acceptance of acupuncture in the United States is an indication of how Chinese medicine can be a useful addition to our overall health care. Pediatric massage is another aspect of Chinese medicine that could be one option in a complete and holistic approach to children's health care.

HOW TO USE THIS BOOK

THIS BOOK IS ORGANIZED AS AN EASILY ACCESSIBLE reference for parents and is written to accommodate parents with varying degrees of interest, from those who want a very simple approach to treating their children to those who want more background information and depth. Some parents will use only the General Health Care massage plan as a means of maintaining good health. Others may also want to learn how to respond to simple colds or coughs, while still others may want to deal with more difficult conditions such as bed-wetting or asthma. You can use this book in all of these cases.

In order to get the most out of this book, I recommend the following process.

GET ACQUAINTED WITH ENERGETIC PRINCIPLES

Before venturing into the techniques or massage plans, take a few minutes to read about energetic principles in chapter 1. Many of the reasons for using certain points or techniques will become clear after you read this very general introduction to Chinese medical concepts. This chapter can also give you an initial sense of the language and concepts used; a glossary of Chinese energetic terminology and a list of recommended reading at the back of the book will give you further information. Later, after you learn about points and techniques, refer back to chapter 1 for clarification. Your understanding of energetic principles will increase as you actually do the massage.

LEARN ABOUT ASSESSMENT SKILLS

Assessment is an important part of choosing the appropriate massage plan. The information presented in chapter 2 is very general and basically requires good observation skills. Knowing these simple skills can provide much information on the energetic health of your child.

PRACTICE THE TECHNIQUES

The techniques used in this book are easy to learn; however, they do require some dexterity and practice. Chapter 3 will explain how to practice the techniques before you use them on your child.

BECOME FAMILIAR WITH THE MASSAGE PLANS

It is useful to look through some of the massage plans in chapter 5 to see how they are organized before you need them. If you are familiar with the basic idea of the massage plans from the start, they will be much easier to use when the situation calls for it.

FEEDBACK OR QUESTIONS

I appreciate any feedback or questions you may have. You may write to me at Kyle Cline, P.O. Box 10714, Portland, OR 97296. You may also reach me by e-mail (kyle@healartspro.com).

Learning about a therapy such as Chinese pediatric massage from a book has limitations. For additional information about other reference books and videos, consult appendix C: Recommended Resources. More detailed and individualized advice can be obtained from qualified practitioners of Chinese medicine.

INTRODUCTION

CHINESE PEDIATRIC MASSAGE (CPM) IS ONE TYPE of therapy used within the framework of traditional Chinese medicine (TCM). TCM consists of three main branches: acupuncture, herbs, and manipulation (or massage). Pediatric massage is a specialty within the manipulation branch of TCM.

Therapeutic massage is capable of influencing a child's energetic flow in the same way that acupuncture works for adults. However, because there are no needles you will find less resistance to and fewer side effects from the massage. CPM is a useful therapy for children from birth to approximately twelve years of age, although it is mainly used for children under six. In general, the younger the child, the more effective these techniques will be.

Massage is one way to use the sophisticated and complete system of Chinese medicine to promote good health and healing in children. While other TCM therapies (notably acupuncture and herbs) may be used, massage is particularly appropriate for children for several reasons. First, children's energy is very accessible. Relative to adults, children have very few barriers or defense mechanisms in place. This results in less need for invasive techniques and consequently less resistance to treatment and fewer side effects. Second, massage involves the very personal, communicative, and bonding process of touch. Using your hands to feel, touch, and massage your child may result in a better response and bonding process. Finally, massage can be performed at home, while traveling, or elsewhere, providing ongoing support for your child generally or for specific conditions.

The purpose of this book is to introduce parents to the home use of this massage system.

It is meant to be a general reference for dealing with common children's conditions, either as a primary therapy or in addition to other medical treatments.

A Brief History of Chinese Pediatric Massage

Pediatric massage, like most aspects of Chinese medicine, evolved slowly but steadily into its present form. As with Chinese medicine as a whole, pediatric massage has gone through a series of phases ranging from flourishing advancement to outright repression and near extinction.

No single date can be conclusively identified as the beginning of Chinese pediatric massage, although the history of Chinese medicine spans approximately three thousand to five thousand years. Few written materials have survived from the early ages.

The earliest surviving written literature on pediatric massage is from the Sui/Tang dynasty (A.D. 581–907). Several books from this era discuss the use of massage techniques for infant conditions. Another series of books has survived from the Song dynasty (960–1279), and during the Yuan dynasty (1279–1368) a pediatric massage department was established at the Institute of the Imperial Physicians.

The Ming dynasty (1368–1644) represents a major period of advancement and flourishing of pediatric massage. At this time pediatric massage was organized into an academic branch within medical institutions and recognized as a specialty practice within the massage profession. Major clinical and theoretical advances occurred, including an independent system of pediatric diagnosis, hand techniques, points, and protocols.

During the Qing dynasty (1644–1911) several pediatric classics were written prior to a change in the political environment, which grew increasingly oppressive to Chinese medicine. Major breakdowns throughout the social, political, and economic systems of China occurred during the Qing dynasty. This also had a significant impact on the practice of medicine. During this time Chinese medicine, not enjoying government support, had little centralized organization and was primarily maintained and taught as a family tradition.

This situation changed significantly after the Communist Revolution (1949), when the government decided to reorganize and promote the use of Chinese medicine. Many scattered and separate pieces of classical Chinese medicine began to be reformed into a coherent whole, which was identified as traditional Chinese medicine (TCM). Pediatric massage was considered a valuable element of TCM and was included in this reorganization. Thus, during the 1950s pediatric massage enjoyed a resurgence in popularity and organizational development.

Chinese history, however, is full of contrasting developments. For example, the advancements made by TCM in the 1950s subsequently suffered a sharp decline during the

Cultural Revolution of the late 1960s and early 1970s. As was the case during the Qing dynasty, although for a much shorter time period, TCM experienced little development in the 60s and 70s. Writing and publishing ceased and many books were destroyed. Teachers and practitioners were barred from their work and forced into other types of labor. It is difficult to know how much was lost during this time, as the Chinese are only now beginning to acknowledge what happened during the Cultural Revolution.

In 1979 the oppression of the Cultural Revolution lifted, and Chinese medicine began slowly to rebuild itself. Pediatric massage continues to this day to be a significant element of the complete system represented by traditional Chinese medicine.

Indications and Contraindications

INDICATIONS: WHEN TO USE MASSAGE

You can use massage for a large variety of pediatric conditions, both acute and chronic. Examples of simple, acute conditions that respond to massage are: colic, common cold, constipation, cough, diarrhea, digestive difficulties, fever, general health care, headache, sore throat, teething, and vomiting.

In addition, some chronic conditions may respond to massage. Examples of chronic conditions include: abdominal distension and pain, asthma, bed-wetting, bronchitis, chicken pox, convulsions, dysentery, earache, hives, jaundice, measles, mumps, night crying, pneumonia, and rubella.

It is important to remember that in some situations a correct assessment and treatment plan must be made by a qualified health care practitioner. In difficult cases massage may be used in conjunction with other types of therapy.

CONTRAINDICATIONS: WHEN NOT TO USE MASSAGE

Knowing when *not* to use massage may be more important than knowing when to use it. The guiding principle behind choosing whether or not to use massage (or any other kind of therapy) is this: First, do no further harm. This is a very commonsense approach to deciding whether massage will be useful. It only takes a few moments to consider the child's condition and whether massage might be harmful. For example, consider a child with abdominal pain, but who also has a skin rash only on the abdomen. In this case, applying massage techniques directly to the abdomen would clearly do more harm than good, although you could still use massage on other areas of the body without aggravating the skin rash.

Simple conditions (such as colds, flu, and diarrhea) usually have no contraindications. If the condition is more complex, however, or if you have any doubts about the situation, consult with a qualified health care practitioner.

No list can cover every possible situation in which massage should not be used. Still, here are some common contraindications for massage in general and pediatric massage in particular (this list is not exhaustive):

- unknown diagnosis
- directly on tumors, acute skin diseases, open wounds, or skin trauma (burns)
- notifiable acute infectious diseases (hepatitis, tuberculosis, diphtheria, typhoid fever)
- internal hemorrhaging
- children taking heavy medication (particularly pain relievers)
- spinal cord trauma

1

CHINESE ENERGETIC PRINCIPLES

BEFORE I GET INTO THE DETAILS OF HOW TO give a pediatric massage, it is important that you have a basic understanding of Chinese energetic principles. Chinese medicine is built on a very different foundation than are Western medical concepts.

The goal of this chapter is to present a simple and understandable version of only the energetic principles you must know to increase your effectiveness in using massage with children. (There is a glossary of terminology at the back of the book.) Specifically, this information will help you choose the most effective points and techniques when performing pediatric massage. This chapter will:

- compare Chinese and Western medicine
- describe Chinese principles of energy
- demonstrate how to apply this information
- list general energetic tendencies of children

There is much more depth and complexity to these concepts than I can present here. If you want to explore this area further, consult appendix C or a practitioner of Chinese medicine.

Chinese Versus Western
Medical Perspectives
氣

As Westerners we have grown up with certain basic assumptions about how we view and understand our bodies. Because most of us in the West have experience only with Western medicine, it can be difficult for us to accept that there are other possible approaches. Understanding these other approaches can be difficult, too, because they use different terminology and descriptions. Still, these approaches, with their different ways of viewing things, can offer new insights and understanding.

Western medicine is focused on the physical aspects of the body. By contrast, Chinese medicine looks at the same body and focuses on energetic flow and balance. It is important to understand the differences between these two approaches. Neither is right or wrong; however, the choice of perspective plays a large role in how we define health and treat disease.

Western medicine has evolved over the past one hundred years with the advances in medical technology. Given the increasing sophistication of observing and measuring material aspects of the human body, Western medicine has become solely focused on its physical aspects.

Chinese medicine, on the other hand, has a continuous history that spans three thousand to five thousand years. Lacking the current technology to explore physical structures, early Chinese doctors sought to explain the function of the human body in energetic terms. For example, Chinese doctors generally did not dissect human cadavers to learn about the internal organs. Instead, they built their theories on the functions they could observe and explained health and disease by a sophisticated system of energy that nourished, supported, and influenced the body's physical structures.

DEFINITIONS OF HEALTH

Because of this difference in focus, Western and Chinese medical systems each operate with different definitions of *health* and *disease*. Western medicine defines *health* as a normal range of physical functioning compared with other people. Western medicine usually does not intervene until a disease process results in significant physical damage. Chinese medicine, however, defines *health* as an optimum balance of energies in the body. Compared to Western medicine, Chinese medicine intervenes much earlier—when signs of imbalance occur and prior to significant physical damage to the body.

Balance is a primary concept of both Western and Chinese medicine. Western medicine looks at the balance of physical aspects; Chinese medicine, at the balance of energetic aspects. Western medicine may focus on the different types of cells in the blood, for instance, and attempt to achieve a balance between white and red blood cells. Chinese medicine may look at different types of energy in the body and attempt to achieve a balance between hot and cold aspects. (Hot and cold energy are explained later on in this chapter.)

Beyond this common interest in balance, however, differences in techniques, application, focus, and intervention appear. One of the major differences between Western and Chinese medicine is that Western medicine only notices that a body is out of balance when there are physical changes that can be measured. For example, when white blood cells increase dramatically above a normal range, Western doctors know the body is trying to fight some kind of infection.

Chinese medicine, however, pays attention to far more subtle energetic signs and attempts to regain balance before physical changes occur. In our previous example, before a blood test would find an elevated white blood cell count, a Chinese doctor would notice signs such as increased heat, fatigue, and perspiration. The Western doctor would describe this process as "the white blood cells increasing to kill the building infection." The Chinese doctor would describe the same situation as "the body's defensive energies gathering to fight off the invading pathogen." Each medical model can thus interpret the same condition in a different way, depending on its focus.

CHOOSING AN APPROPRIATE MODEL

Any medical model is only as useful as it is helpful in describing and treating a condition of the human body. What is sometimes difficult to grasp is that a single medical model is not necessarily best at describing every medical condition.

For example, the Western medical model is very effective when there is significant physical damage to the body. During a heart attack, Western medicine intervenes with drug therapy and possibly surgery to correct the obstructed flow of blood to the heart. In many cases this is a lifesaving procedure. Before the obvious physical signs of a heart attack appear, however, Western medicine is less effective. Chinese medicine can observe more subtle signs of an energetic imbalance related to the heart and attempt to correct this before damage occurs.

The different perspectives of each model lead to different areas of effectiveness. We need not rely on one model to describe every condition; it is more useful to choose the most appropriate model for the condition. *The most appropriate model is the one that best describes and treats the condition.*

Both Western and Chinese medical methodologies offer useful ways of dealing with health and disease. The Western perspective is very useful at dramatic, lifesaving, invasive procedures when there is serious physical damage in the body. Surgery and drug therapy are two good examples of such Western medical expertise. If you need surgery to correct a heart imbalance, Western medicine is the most appropriate method. Chinese medicine, on the other hand, is more focused on trying to deal with imbalances before they require deeply invasive measures. Thus, this perspective uses more subtle assessment techniques and therapies.

In *Between Heaven and Earth* Harriet Beinfield and Efrem Korngold compare the Western medical doctor with a mechanic and the Chinese medical doctor with a gardener. The mechanic focuses on replacing deteriorating parts only when they have reached a point of major malfunction. The gardener strives to avoid major problems in the garden through a good environment, including nourishment from the soil, sun, and water. Both perspectives can be valuable when used appropriately.

The Chinese Medical Perspective— Understanding Qi
氣

The beauty of Chinese medicine lies in its ability to distinguish among subtly different levels of conditions and use techniques or therapies specific to the level. This ability to distinguish different types of energetic patterns within a similar condition is a valuable tool because the treatment can be much more refined and targeted. For example, in the West we think of the common cold as caused by a virus, and we treat all colds similarly. In Chinese medicine the common cold can be broken down into several types depending on energetic factors, such as heat, wind, cold, and damp.

The Chinese term used to describe the various types of energies in our bodies is *qi*. This term (sometimes spelled *chi*) is much more refined than the English word *energy*. Qi is a very subtle vibration that can be felt but not seen or measured.

Because energetic terminology, like *qi*, is somewhat difficult to grasp, the use of analogies can be helpful. Remember that an analogy is not an exact description but a picture that helps explain the concept.

In general, the qi in our bodies can be compared with the flow of water. Water flows through a region via lakes, rivers, and streams. A "balanced water flow," then, describes a good, normal amount of water flowing throughout the region, with no flooding or drought in any area. The cleanliness of the water is also a factor; water that is stagnant or blocked, or that does not flow well, becomes unclean and tends to develop problems.

For the general good health of the region it is important to have enough volume and good circulation of clean water.

Qi circulates through the body in much the same way as water. Having enough qi and a good flow of qi are the general ingredients of good health. When there is a problem with the quantity, quality, or flow of qi, the beginnings of disease occur.

Again, the water analogy can be useful. If by chance a large log were to fall across a stream, it would block the water flow. What would happen?

At first, the results would not be obviously bad. The stream would continue to flow; however, the water would begin to back up behind the log. Although there is nothing wrong with this, over time it could worsen. The basic imbalance is an impeded flow, which creates too much water upstream from the log and too little downstream. The problems that could develop if this situation were left unchanged include flooding; stagnant water, which would result in an increase in bacteria and algae, possibly disrupting the local food chain; and not enough water downstream, leading to vegetation drying out and the loss of habitat for insects and wildlife.

In the body qi can also be blocked—its flow through the body impeded. These blockages are defined in energetic terms, such as "too much heat, cold, damp, or the like hindering the flow of qi through an area." The degree of impact that such blockages have can vary greatly, from a very slight disruption of energetic flow to a major disruption. *The goal in Chinese medicine is to deal with the imbalance at a very subtle and early stage, before stagnation and major physical symptoms develop.*

The focus of treatment is to encourage the flow of qi. This can be done in a variety of ways, from boosting the level of qi (adding water to the stream) to removing blockages that impede the flow of qi.

Returning to our stream analogy, after the log blocking the stream is removed the water begins flowing again and eventually restores balance to the area, decreasing flooding, relieving drought, and purifying the water. Thus the saying, "Running water purifies itself." In the case of the human body, a major way to help the body regain balance is to promote a good flow of qi; the body will then purify itself of any stuck or imbalanced energies. This is the focus of Chinese medicine.

Energetic Physiology—
An Energetic Perspective of the Body
氣

Let's examine some more detailed information about how qi is produced in the body, how it flows around the body, and the energetic factors that influence this flow.

What Each Child Has to Begin With:
Energetic Constitution

We each inherit a basic energetic constitution at birth in the same way that we inherit physical characteristics from our parents. This is the foundation level of qi that we have to build and grow with. Constitutional energetics set the foundation from which all other energies develop.

Like inherited physical characteristics, constitutional energies vary from person to person. Some people inherit a very balanced constitution; some start off with weaknesses in certain areas. If there are apparent weaknesses, these areas will need extra attention.

Just because an energetic constitution may be weak, however, does not mean immediate or inevitable problems. Constitutional weaknesses can be strengthened, although the degree of improvement will depend on the relative degree of weakness.

How Children Create Energy:
Qi Production

Chinese medical theory views the organ systems as the major producers and controllers of qi. In the same way that Western medicine assigns physiological tasks to each organ (such as the liver filtering toxins and purifying blood), Chinese medicine assigns energetic functions to each organ.

Each organ system includes the physical structure of the organ, all of the points related to that organ along its meridian (pathways that qi flows through), and the energetic function of the organ throughout the body. For example, the liver organ system includes the physical structure of the liver in the upper right area of the abdomen; the liver meridian, which runs from the big toe up the inside of the leg and into the abdomen on both sides of the body; fourteen major points along the liver meridian; and the energetic function of "spreading," or providing for the smooth flow of qi, blood, fluids, emotions, and other energies throughout the body. In the context of Chinese medicine the term *liver* refers to this whole intricate system.

Each of the organ systems is responsible for different aspects of qi production or movement. The following paragraphs give a brief description of each organ system and its primary qi-production role. The accompanying chart summarizes these functions.

ORGAN SYSTEM CHARACTERISTICS

YIN ORGAN	YANG PARTNER	QI-PRODUCTION ROLE	EMOTIONS	RELATED BODY PARTS/TISSUES
Lung	Large intestine	Draw qi from air while breathing	Courage/sadness	Nose/skin
Kidney	Bladder	Store pre- and postnatal qi	Gentleness/fear	Ear/bone
Liver	Gallbladder	Spread qi smoothly through body	Kindness/anger	Eye/tendons
Heart	Small intestine	Spirit/direction of qi	Joy/impatience	Tongue/blood vessels
Spleen	Stomach	Transform food into qi	Harmony/worry	Mouth/muscles

LUNGS

The lungs are responsible for transforming the air taken into the body through breathing into usable qi for the body.

KIDNEYS

The kidneys are responsible for storing and releasing qi when it is needed by the body. Two major types of qi are stored in the kidneys: prenatal qi and postnatal qi. Prenatal qi is the energy you inherit from both parents at birth. This genetic qi determines your basic characteristics and energetic constitution. It is a very pure and powerful form of qi and should be conserved. The amount of prenatal qi you have basically determines the length and quality of your life.

Postnatal qi is the qi you produce after birth from such daily activities as eating, breathing, meditation, and exercise. Postnatal qi that is not consumed during the daily function of your body is stored in the kidneys for future use. The body normally draws on postnatal qi to fill demands, but will access prenatal qi when postnatal qi is unavailable. The ideal is to have a strong daily production of postnatal qi so that your prenatal qi will rarely be accessed.

LIVER

The liver is responsible for the smooth flow of qi throughout the body so that all aspects are nourished properly. This includes nourishing the organs (spleen, lungs, etc.) more directly involved in qi production so that they produce abundant qi.

HEART

This organ is responsible for providing the overall direction and spirit of qi in the body. The heart plays a role similar to that of the classical Chinese emperor. The emperor gave direction and spiritual counsel to the entire country through his ministers, who were each responsible for a specific function. In the body the heart provides overall direction, which the other organ systems carry out through their specific responsibilities.

SPLEEN

The spleen is responsible for transforming food into usable qi for the body. This responsibility includes both digestion and elimination.

Qi is produced and moved throughout the body by the interrelated functioning of all of these organ systems.

How Qi Circulates Throughout the Body: Qi Distribution

Meridians are the means for moving qi around the body so that it can do its work. The meridians are the vessels, or pathways, that conduct qi to all aspects of the body. These meridians are integral parts of the organ systems described above. The primary meridians are associated with each of the primary organs and are also named for them—for example, the liver meridian is named for the liver organ.

Along the path of the meridian are specific points that can affect the related organ, the energetic function of this organ, and the flow of qi through the meridian and the associated region. Using our previous water analogy, the meridians are similar to rivers, which transport water from lakes and mountain springs throughout the region. A point on a meridian is similar to a place on a river where the water can be influenced to flow in a certain way.

Describing Qi: Eight Principles of Energetic Balance

With a basic understanding of qi and how it flows through the body, we can start to discriminate among different types of energy and their relative balance.

The Eight Principles help explain the relative balance of energies among four pairs of opposite, yet complementary, energies: yin and yang, deficient and excessive, interior and exterior, and cold and hot. I will briefly describe each of these pairs to provide a framework for understanding the nature of a particular imbalance.

YIN AND YANG

Yin and *yang* are Chinese terms used to describe the basic polarities of opposing energies. Yin represents the aspects that are contracting and at rest; yang, the aspects that are expanding and active. Together they represent the whole spectrum of relative energetic balances.

YIN/YANG CHARACTERISTICS	
YIN	**YANG**
Rest	Action
Contraction	Expansion
Descension	Ascension
Cool	Warm
Moist	Dry
Heavy	Light
Inside	Outside
Small	Large
Soft	Hard

The value of these concepts lies in being able to describe a quality by relating it to its opposite. For example, when it comes to gender, men are considered more yang relative to women, who are more yin. However, one man may be considered more yin when compared to another man, who is more yang. It is important to understand that yin and yang are not absolute labels of things, nor are they judgments of good or bad, right or wrong. Yin/yang is a way of describing the relative types of energies that characterize a person, thing, or condition.

General signs and symptoms can also be categorized as being predominantly yin or yang.

YIN/YANG SIGNS	
YIN	**YANG**
Quiet	Talkative
Slow	Rapid movement
Tired	Agitated
Feels cold	Feels hot
Chronic	Acute

In addition, yin and yang can be used to describe energetic conditions in a very general manner. The remaining three pairs of principles are categorized as being predominantly yin or yang.

YIN/YANG PRINCIPLES	
YIN	YANG
Deficient	Excessive
Interior	Exterior
Cold	Hot

These remaining three pairs can further discriminate among the relative balances of energy in terms of strength (deficient and excessive), location (interior and exterior), and temperature (cold and hot).

STRENGTH

Excessive and *deficient* describe the relative differences in strength or quantity of qi in a condition. Returning to our example of a stream blocked by a log, the area upstream of the log would be called "excessive" of water, while the area downstream would be called "deficient." The various problems downstream (lack of water, dying vegetation, parched earth, fewer insects and animals, etc.) could be collectively described as a "deficient water condition." The various problems upstream (flooding, stagnation, algae, unclean water, etc.) are described as an "excessive water condition."

The same is true for energy in the body. If there is poor flow in an area or a blockage along the flow of a meridian, the area upstream will generally be excessive and the area downstream deficient.

We can also use these terms to describe a general condition based on the overall signs and symptoms. For example, someone with a condition that included feeling cold, being lethargic, and sleeping more than usual would be characterized as having a deficient energy condition. A person whose condition included a fever, agitation, and restlessness would be characterized as having an excessive energy condition.

LOCATION

Another way to describe an energetic pattern is in terms of the depth of the energetic imbalance relative to the *interior* or *exterior*. These terms help identify at what level the energetic balance is disturbed. An example of an exterior pattern is when energy from the environment penetrates and begins to affect the body's function, such as with a common cold. Here, cold is affecting the balance of energy at the surface, causing surface symptoms: sneezing, chills, cough, and so on. An interior pattern involves a disruption at a much deeper level. For example, if the cold worsens it could move deeper into the body, affecting the lungs and causing bronchitis or pneumonia.

TEMPERATURE

In the final category the terms *heat* and *cold* are used to describe the relative differences in temperature displayed in a pattern. For example, a common cold that includes a high fever, extreme thirst, or redness in the face would be categorized as a heat pattern. A cold that includes chills but no fever, thirst, or sweating would be categorized as a cold pattern.

With a basic understanding of the Eight Principles, you can identify a particular energetic pattern according to these different levels. For example, one common cold pattern would be identified as excessive heat in the exterior. These terms help you identify the relative types of energies involved and where they are, and therefore, tell you how to focus the treatment.

Environmental Energetic Aspects: Six External Pathogenic Factors

Another method to describe the energetics of a pattern is to look at environmental factors that may influence it. This concept is called the Six External Pathogenic Factors. These six environmental energies—heat, cold, damp, wind, dry, and summer heat—can affect the internal energy of the body. For example, cold weather can suddenly drain the body of warmth, changing its overall temperature balance to be colder. This pattern would be identified as having an external cold cause. The treatment would be to offset the excess of cold with warmth, strengthen the exterior to prevent the cold from penetrating, and open the exterior to disperse the external cold energy outward.

How Energetic Theories Help Identify a Pattern
氣

With all of the above terms to help us describe the energetic nature of a pattern, we can begin to create an assessment of what precisely is out of balance. This helps determine what type of therapy, techniques, or points are necessary to help restore energetic balance, which in turn encourages the body to do what it does naturally.

To further clarify how all these theories are used, consider a simple case of diarrhea and how it might be described in energetic terms. Identifying that a child has diarrhea does not identify the cause, which may be any of several factors. Western medicine distinguishes among diarrhea caused by stomach flu, bad food, and irritable bowels. However, Chinese medicine continues to break down the possible types and energetic causes into more subtle distinctions. In mild cases of children's diarrhea, for example, there are typically four major energetic patterns: cold or damp, heat, improper eating, and fragile spleen.

Even though all of these patterns result in diarrhea, their energetic aspects differ. The signs and symptoms show how these patterns differ:

> Cold or damp diarrhea: Pale complexion and lips, no thirst or mouth dryness, aversion to cold, cold limbs
> Heat diarrhea: Sudden onset, thirst, hot body feeling, perspiration
> Improper eating diarrhea: Abdominal distension and pain, relief after bowel movement, recent history of overeating or improper diet
> Fragile-spleen diarrhea: Recurrent diarrhea, undigested food in stool, abdominal fullness, no thirst, emaciation, listlessness, lethargy

The energetic description is your guide to choosing which techniques and points to use. For example, in the above case of cold or damp diarrhea, choose points that are warming in nature and those that dispel dampness. If you were treating a case of heat diarrhea, though, the use of these same points would increase warmth in a pattern that was already too warm, resulting in a worsening of the condition. This is the practical value of identifying the proper energetic pattern.

The massage plans in this book help you identify the type of pattern (for example, cold, hot, or fragile-spleen diarrhea) and then, under the heading Variations, provide different techniques and points for each pattern (see the Diarrhea massage plan on pages 96–97).

Children's General Energetic Tendencies
氣

The information I've given you so far on energetic principles is general and can be applied to both adults and children. Now I will turn to energetic tendencies commonly seen in infants and children. The following descriptions are general tendencies only; each child must be evaluated on an individual basis.

Inherent Organ Deficiencies and Excesses

The growth and development of a child's energetic system is similar to that of the structural and physiological systems. At birth these systems are immature, yet functional at a level necessary for continued growth and development. The younger the child, the more immature the energetic system, and the greater the difference from that of an adult.

The meridians demonstrate the difference between children and adults. Adult meridians extend from either the hands or the feet to the torso. Meridians in children are not fully developed and are found only in the fingers of each hand (see figures 1 and 2).

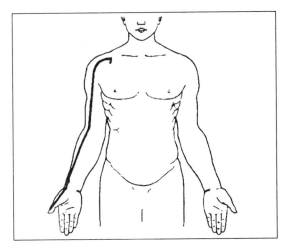

FIG. 1: ADULT LUNG MERIDIAN

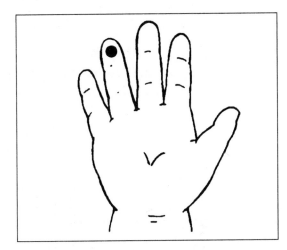

FIG. 2: CHILD LUNG MERIDIAN

As a parent you must realize that a child is not simply a smaller version of an adult, nor do all children present a single energetic picture. The term *child* covers a wide spectrum of ages: from birth through twelve years old. Unless specifically identified, the word *child* in this book is used in this general way.

Let's look at the deficiencies and excesses that are inherent and normal in children's immature energetic systems. All the information in this section should be adapted to fit the age, size, and energetic nature of the individual child.

What Happens with Too Little Energy: Inherent Organ Deficiencies

Due to their rapidly developing bodies, children consume large amounts of qi. Therefore, the organs most responsible for producing qi—the spleen, lungs, and kidneys—are frequently in a deficient state because of this high demand and need. Prior to the child's birth, the mother's organs were responsible for providing the qi necessary for growth and development. At birth this large demand is shifted solely to the child's organs, which are not energetically mature. The deficiencies of these organs can produce the following conditions:

> Spleen: With additional stress, the already deficient spleen will manifest in digestive and elimination disorders such as gastrointestinal difficulties, abdominal pain or distension, vomiting, diarrhea, and malabsorption. A weak digestive process is probably the most common energetic pattern seen in children from birth through approximately four to six years old.
>
> Lungs: Attacked by strong environmental energies, the deficient lungs easily develop respiratory disorders such as the common cold, coughing, sneezing, and runny nose. Greater stress placed on the lungs may produce bronchitis, asthma, wheezing, and pneumonia.
>
> Kidneys: Without proper care or nourishment, the deficient kidneys may worsen until they cannot support their role in growth, resulting in developmental disorders such as muscle atrophy, flaccidity, and delayed growth patterns.

What Happens with Too Much Energy: Inherent Excessive Energies

In addition to inherently deficient organs, children naturally have excesses in the heart and liver organs and yang qi in general. These three inherent excesses reflect the hyperactive energy required for physiological and energetic growth and development. Remember, this is a natural consequence of the massive changes under way in their bodies.

The physical and energetic development of a child is very demanding. The general motivating force behind this transformation is excessive yang and liver qi. This transformative process of growth and development requires large amounts of yang qi (very active, expanding, upward and outward movement) to guide the process. Although necessary, these natural excesses may become extreme and result in the conditions detailed here:

Liver qi: With additional stress, excessive liver qi may cause imbalances in the smooth flow of a child's energies. A good example is the flow of emotions. Quick and strong emotional behaviors, such as shouting and anger, reflect a liver qi condition. Excessive liver qi imbalances usually present as blockages in the smooth flow of energy, such as headaches, uncontrollable temper or anger, disturbed sleep, irritability, nervous tics, or convulsions.

Yang qi: Overabundance of yang qi is a general condition that does not in itself manifest as any particular condition, but does have a strong influence on the nature and course of most conditions. The quick, dramatic onset and adaptability of most conditions in children is related to the highly active nature of excessive yang qi.

Heart qi: Described as the "spirit" of the child, heart qi plays a pivotal role in physical and energetic development by providing guidance and direction for growth. At birth and through early childhood, the heart qi is very strong relative to physical development. This leads to a basic imbalance, because the strength of the heart is not grounded in the physical body.

A good example of this is seen in children just before they can crawl. They are very active (excessive qi) but do not quite have the ability to move the way they want (physical capacity). This frequently results in frustration (imbalance), which may manifest in different ways. Having a large amount of yang qi without a corresponding ground for that qi can result in imbalances.

In the case of unstable heart qi, the manifestations are easily seen in the quickly shifting emotions of a child. Children can easily and quickly shift from one extreme emotion to another, like the wind on a blustery day. This is a normal aspect of childhood and should not be considered a problem needing treatment (although it may be difficult to deal with). Other normal examples of unstable heart qi include a short attention span and self-centeredness.

One additional aspect of unstable heart qi is the relative ease with which it can be startled. Extreme fright is particularly unsettling to the heart, which is already unstable. Chinese pediatricians view fright as a potential causative factor in many energetic imbalances, which should be minimized whenever possible.

Excessive and unstable heart qi can affect any other organ and result in almost any type of condition. Common examples include night crying, extreme emotional behaviors, and digestion and elimination disorders.

Quick Recovery and
Response to Treatment
氣

In general, children are full of vitality; when imbalanced their reactions are sensitive and prompt. The predominance of yang (active qi) in children is responsible for the rapid development of and changes in an illness. It is also responsible for their vigorous growth, development, and ability to recover quickly.

Relative to adults' diseases, children's diseases are often simpler, showing less variety in signs, emotional swings, and multiple disease patterns. Because of their vigorous physiological functions, children may quickly marshal strong internal energetic resources. Given appropriate care when ill, all of these factors may contribute to a rapid recovery and response to treatment by massage.

2
ASSESSMENT

IT IS USEFUL TO TAKE TIME TO ASSESS almost any situation before taking action. All of us perform some kind of assessment in many daily activities. For example, if certain plants in the garden are not thriving, a gardener first completes a general assessment. Is the soil too dry, too wet, compacted? Is there enough light, or too much light? Are there pests involved?

Sometimes the assessment stage is so routine that we do not realize we are doing it. In the case of using pediatric massage it is very important to make assessment a conscious step in the process. The information you gather during the assessment stage will tell you the energetic nature of your child's pattern. Once that is established, you can perform massage according to the plans in chapter 5.

Assessment means gathering information about the child that gives clues about the energetic characteristics of his or her pattern. In Western medicine, assessment skills are mostly very technical in nature (blood tests, X-rays, EKGs, etc.). Chinese medical assessment relies less on technology and more on sensory skills. These skills can be divided into four general categories: looking, asking, listening, and feeling.

One of the major benefits of Chinese assessment techniques is the ability to notice subtle signs of imbalance and respond to them before they become major signs of imbalance. For example, with a child who has a history of chronic ear infections, the ability to recognize very early signs of a cold can lead to prompt attention and care, which may forestall the occurrence of another ear infection. Prevention is a crucial aspect of Chinese medicine.

Learning these assessment skills should be easy. With them you can identify the practical signs and symptoms you can see in your child and also apply the energetic information you learned in the last chapter. The assessment skills presented here are very basic and do not require professional training to use. There are, however, other assessment skills within Chinese medicine that take many years of education and practice to master, such as pulse taking. Also, many of the simple skills presented here, such as tongue diagnosis, can be used with much more depth by professionals.

The assessment skills presented in this chapter are intended to help you understand simple patterns of energetic imbalance. They are not a guide for diagnosis or medical treatment. When necessary, consult with a qualified health care practitioner.

Looking

Observation of a child plays an important role in overall assessment because energetic imbalances are easily reflected at the surface. Paying close attention to the tongue, complexion, and the point named *Mountain Base* will provide useful information.

TONGUE

The tongue is a very expressive part of the body energetically. It is used extensively throughout Chinese medicine to provide detailed information about internal balances of excess and deficiency, heat and cold. Examine the table (below) for common signs and their associated energetic patterns.

TONGUE	
SIGN	PATTERN
Light red, free motion, moist	Normal
Delicate, tender, moves easily	Normal
Thin white coat	Normal
Pale	Qi and blood deficiency
Bright red	Interior heat
Deep red, crimson	Internal pathogenic heat
White, thick	Damp, phlegm
Very moist	Cold, damp
Dry yellow coat	Excess internal heat, depleted fluids
Gray thin coat	Light external pathogenic invasion
Thick black coat	Strong external pathogenic invasion
Purple	Qi and blood stagnation
Thin white coat	External pathogenic invasion, cold
White, sticky	Internal cold and damp

SIGN	PATTERN
Yellow, sticky	Damp heat, turbid damp in abdomen
Greasy yellow	Damp, phlegm
Dry peeled coat	Deficient yin, fluid exhaustion
Pale red with scattered spots	Flaring heart fire
Swollen, rigid	Convulsion
Scorched yellow	Heat stagnation
Black	Extreme cold or heat, deep penetration of body
White border, dry coat, black center	Critical condition

It takes some time and practice to recognize different signs on the tongue. Adequate natural light is necessary; tongue signs can be subtle. Still, while practitioners may make a detailed tongue assessment, parents can use it in a very general way. For example, noticing whether the tongue is unusually pale or red will indicate if the child's condition is cold or hot. That may be the extent of detail you need to choose the appropriate massage plan.

One good way to gain skill in tongue assessment is to look at your child's tongue frequently. With repetition, you can establish what looks normal when the child is healthy. A significant change in the tongue indicates that an energetic imbalance is occurring.

The tongue can also be used as a guide for the organ or part of the body involved in the pattern of disharmony. Chinese medical theory states that the entire body is reflected by the tongue, which is why it is such a good assessment area. Each area of the tongue corresponds to specific internal organs (see figure 3). Signs of imbalance in a specific region usually relate to the corresponding organ. For example, a normal-looking tongue with a raised patch of moist white fur in the center indicates cold and damp in the spleen area. This sign would generally correspond to some type of digestion or elimination condition. Another example is a normal tongue with a significant red area at the tip. The redness indicates excess heat, and the tip of the tongue corresponds to the heart organ. Therefore, this sign indicates excess heart qi, many times brought on by overstimulation. In

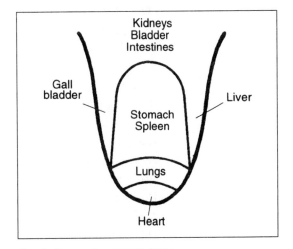

FIG. 3: TONGUE ASSESSMENT AREAS

children the most notable organ regions of the tongue to look for are the spleen or stomach, heart, and lungs.

COMPLEXION

Colors of the complexion are useful for distinguishing between excess and deficiency, hot and cold. Adequate natural light is necessary to perceive subtle differences in color.

COMPLEXION	
SIGN	PATTERN
Blue	Liver
Red	Heart heat
Yellow	Spleen
White	Lungs
Green	Wind, liver, or deficient stomach/spleen
Dark, black	Kidneys
Blue face	Convulsions
Flushed face	Excess heat
Yellow face	Indigestion, impaired spleen, damp, weak constitution
White face	Deficiency, cold
Dark face	Severe pain
Yellow-red	Yang heat
Yellow with yellow sclera	Jaundice
Dim black	Congenital deficiency or cold accumulation and obstruction
Black or purplish blue below lower lip	Convulsion
Pale	Cold, deficiency
Pale and pale lips	Blood deficiency
Pale with perspiration	Deficient lung and defensive qi
Pale, sallow	Spleen deficiency
Pale, glossy	Qi deficiency
Purplish blue complexion and lips	Strong liver wind or cold abdominal pain
Purplish blue, twitch, fright, palpitation	Convulsion
Purplish blue, fast breathing	Qi stagnation, blood stasis
Red, flushed	Fever

Complexion color is a useful way to narrow down the range of possible energetic patterns. For example, if a child is paler than normal the energetic pattern would relate to some form of deficiency. A child who is redder than normal has a general excess pattern. Combining the information from complexion with other signs can lead from general to more specific energetic information.

MOUNTAIN BASE

Mountain Base is located just above the bridge of the nose and between the eyebrows (see figure 4). This area is a good indicator of the condition of the spleen, which generally relates to digestion or elimination. This assessment is most useful for infants and children under six years old.

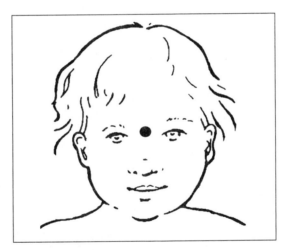

FIG. 4: MOUNTAIN BASE

MOUNTAIN BASE	
SIGN	PATTERN
Blue vein	Spleen deficiency.
Bluish tint	Initial stage of developing spleen-deficiency pattern
Black	Kidney wind, cold
Pale	Accumulated phlegm in lungs
Purplish blue	Liver wind

A change in *Mountain Base* is a very useful sign to watch for. The gradual appearance of a slight bluish tint can be an early indicator of an approaching problem. This will usually be a digestion or elimination problem, but is not restricted to these conditions.

Asking

The asking phase of assessment will vary according to the age of the child. Depending on their ability to communicate and their reliability, children can provide useful information that will assist in the assessment process. Asking may also be an appropriate process for care providers other than the parent who may have been with the child during the progression of the condition.

TEMPERATURE

Information on temperature helps you distinguish the type and seriousness of external pathogenic invasions.

TEMPERATURE	
SIGN	PATTERN
Prefers cold	Heat
Prefers heat	Cold
Fever, chills, no or spontaneous sweating, wind aversion	Wind, cold, external pathogenic invasion
Constant feverish body and palms	Deficient yin, internal injury
Fever, chills, absence of perspiration	Wind, cold, external pathogenic invasion
Fever, wind aversion, perspiration	Wind, heat, external pathogenic invasion
Alternating chills and fever	Half-exterior, half-interior
Summertime, protracted high fever, thirst	Summer heat
Feeble limbs, gray complexion, pale lips, spontaneous sweating, slight aversion to cold	Yang deficiency
Chills, absence of fever	Internal cold, deficient yang
Lassitude, glossy pale complexion, pale lips, spontaneous perspiration, slight aversion to cold	Deficient yang, fever

In extreme conditions the hot or cold nature of the child is very obvious. In more subtle situations, however, it may be difficult to ascertain temperature. One easy method in this situation is to notice the child's desire for hot or cold drinks, and more or less clothing or bedding.

URINE AND STOOL

Qualities of urine and stool are indicators of the functioning of the spleen (digestion and elimination system) and whether the pattern is excessive or deficient, hot or cold.

URINE AND STOOL	
SIGN	**PATTERN**
Yellow stool, neither too hard or moist	Normal
Clear, light-yellow urine	Normal
Scanty, deep-colored urine, hot weather	Normal
Loose stool, diarrhea	Deficiency
Frequent urination, bed-wetting	Deficient kidney qi
Brown urine	Heat
Deep yellow-red urine	Damp, heat
Clear urine, no odor	Cold, spleen or kidney deficiency
Sticky, foul stool	Heat
Watery, foul stool	Cold
Constipation with heat signs	Yang stagnation
Constipation with cold signs	Cold stagnation
Watery diarrhea, foul mucous stools, burning anus, heat signs	Excess heat
Brown diarrhea, scanty urine	Damp heat
Dry stool, sheep droppings with several days of no stool	Excess heat in intestines, yin deficiency, fluid exhaustion
Loose stool, fetid odor	Stagnant interior damp, heat
Incessant, watery diarrhea with undigested food	Spleen or kidney deficiency
Pale, watery, frothy diarrhea	External pathogenic wind, cold
Red, white, sticky, jellylike stool	Damp, heat accumulation
Dark red stool with crying fits	Intestinal obstruction
Dry stool, constipation	Interior deficient yin, heat
Sour, fetid, loose stool	Improper feeding
Constipation at early stage of condition	Excess heat in large intestine
Constipation, prolonged illness	Depletion of body fluids
Frequent, loose stools	Spleen deficiency
Clear, dilute, rotten-fish stool	Cold
Dysentery, pus and blood in stool	Excess heat in large intestine

The quality and frequency of elimination patterns can also serve as early indicators of a developing condition. This is particularly true with infants or toddlers still in diapers. When their stools begin to change from a normal consistency, watch for other signs and provide extra care. For example, the stools of children who are susceptible to colds and earaches will frequently become loose before other obvious signs of a cold are present. Dealing with the condition when the stool becomes loose is much easier than when it has turned into a full-blown earache.

PERSPIRATION

The degree of perspiration indicates the depth and relative strength of a condition.

PERSPIRATION	
SIGN	PATTERN
Slight forehead sweat while sleeping	Normal
No sweating, fever, chill	Exterior, excess
Sweating, fever, chill	Exterior, deficiency
Lassitude, sweating with exertion	Yang deficiency
Sweating, chill	Exterior
Sweating, no chill, fever, heat aversion	Interior
Spontaneous daytime sweat with slight exertion	Qi deficiency
Night sweats	Yin deficiency, qi and yin deficiency
Spontaneous, profuse daytime sweating	Deficient qi and weak defensive qi
Profuse, continuous sweating	Yang exhaustion, potential collapse

The degree of perspiration is a surface indication of internal energetic dynamics. In general, the main sign to look for is the presence or absence of perspiration. However, the time of perspiration can provide more subtle information. For example, the presence of sweating usually indicates a deficient, exterior condition while the absence of sweating indicates an exterior, excessive condition. Sweating only at night indicates an internal deficiency that is much deeper and must be treated at the deeper level.

DIET

Information on diet can tell you the quality of a child's nourishment, possible beginnings of his or her condition, and overall functioning of his or her spleen.

DIET	
SIGN	PATTERN
Hunger, no appetite, stomach distress	Stomach obstruction, phlegm, heat
Increased food intake, hunger, weight loss	Flaming stomach fire
Good appetite, abdominal distension	Weak spleen and strong stomach
Abdominal distension after eating	Qi stagnation and indigestion
Stomachache, abdominal pain relieved after eating	Deficiency
Stomachache, pain worse after eating	Excess
Prefers hot food	Cold stomach and intestines
Prefers cold food	Hot stomach and intestines
Poor appetite, abdominal fullness or distension	Excess, food stagnation
Excessive eating and stools, emaciation	Hyperfunction of stomach or spleen (malnutrition)
Appetite loss, constipation, frequent belching	Food stagnation

It is normal for infants and children to go through many changes in appetite and eating habits. However, when their habits begin to change outside of their normal patterns, it may be an early indicator of a potential problem. For example, a child who generally eats a variety of things but suddenly desires only cold foods may have a heat condition in the digestive system.

Listening

Listening to the quality of the sounds that your child makes and of your child's voice can provide supplementary assessment information about the type of energetic pattern involved (see table on following page).

Because children are so expressive with their voices, it is relatively easy to discern changes by this method. For example, a normally exuberant and talkative child who becomes quiet and withdrawn may be showing signs of a deficient or cold energetic condition.

VOICE AND SOUNDS

SIGN	PATTERN
Clear loud speech	Normal
Muffled voice (strong then feeble)	External pathogenic invasion
Not talkative, cold	Deficiency
Crying with profuse tears	Excess
Feeble voice, low tones	Qi deficiency, kidney
Shouting, scolding	Pain, liver
Trembling sound	Spleen
Giggling, flat speech	Heart
Frowning, groaning	Headache
Loud groaning, touching chest	Stomach
Groaning, shaking head, touching cheeks	Toothache
Groaning, failing to stand	Low back pain
Feeble crying, weak voice	Deficiency
Coughing, coarse voice, productive mucus, nasal obstruction	Wind, cold, external pathogenic invasion
Chronic cough, hoarse voice	Deficient lung qi
Coughing, hoarse voice, sounds like splintering wood	Laryngitis, diphtheria
Deep harsh cough, sticky yellow phlegm	External wind, heat
Cough with clear loud sound and clear nasal discharge	External wind, cold
Paroxysmal cough, whoops with inspiration	Whooping cough
Dry cough	Lung dryness
Hoarse voice	Throat or vocal chord disorders, internal accumulated wind, phlegm, heat
Crying with tears	Excess
Crying without tears	Deficiency
Crying not alleviated by normal methods, on and off, shrill, unhurried then anxious	Abdominal pain
Crying with shaking head and heat	Head pain
Crying with refusing food, slobbering	Mouth ulcers
Talkative, fever	Yang excess
Reluctant speech, coldness	Yin deficiency
Loud voice	Excess, external pathogenic invasion
Shrill shout	Severe pain
Fluent cough with free phlegm discharge	Mild condition

Touching

Relative to adults, children have an open and accessible body structure. They have fewer defensive barriers and less density to their bodies. Thus, the skill of touching can provide useful assessment information. I will describe touching used on the abdominal area to help in the assessment process.

ABDOMEN	
SIGN	PATTERN
Soft, tender, warm abdomen	Normal
Soft abdomen, pain relieved by pressure	Deficient, cold
Hard abdomen, pain aggravated by pressure	Excess, heat
Sharp pain, hard abdomen	Excess
Prefers warmth	Cold
Prefers cold	Heat
Distended abdomen, shallow sensation with pressure	Gas distension
Liquid sounds in abdomen	Liquid accumulation
Tossing and turning, shouting, or crying while holding abdomen	Abdominal pain
Tough, scorching abdomen	Accumulation and stagnation in intestines
Abdominal distension with tapping sounds like a drum	Stagnant qi

The smaller the child, the greater the proportion of the abdomen to the entire body. This is a good opportunity to evaluate an easily accessible area of the body. For example, the degree of softness or hardness of the abdomen signifies the relative deficient or excess energy of the condition.

CONCLUSION

The development of Chinese medicine occurred prior to the evolution of sophisticated technology for assessing the human body. Thus, Chinese physicians developed assessment skills that could provide information on the internal environment through simple observation. Over centuries of practice these observational skills became highly refined.

While Western medical assessment is highly technical and quantitative, Chinese medical assessment is more an art form. The ability to see and recognize subtle signs is an important aspect of this art. It is important to look at all of the available assessment signs and symptoms before you reach a conclusion on the energetic pattern. For example, it is not wise to make a decision based on just the appearance of the tongue. You must consider all of the relevant information as a whole.

In some ways energetic assessment is like painting a landscape picture: many colors and details together create the picture. Each sign or symptom provides one piece of the overall picture—in this case the energetic pattern of the child.

A NOTE OF CAUTION

I have presented the information in this chapter in a basic format. However, children do not always conform to a basic energetic pattern. Don't let this deter you from using the assessment process, but do be aware that assessing a particular combination of signs and symptoms is not always simple. The more experience you have, the easier it will be to read these energetic signs and interpret the pattern.

These assessment skills are not limited to use when your child is ill. They may be applied at any time and may give you useful information to prevent illness from occurring. Careful observation and regular applications of the General Health Care massage plan (see page 103) are together a good way to maintain health.

The assessment skills presented here are only a few of those used in Chinese medicine. Practitioners are trained to look for more subtle and detailed information. If you have any questions, consult a trained professional.

3
TECHNIQUES

A PROFESSIONAL MASSAGE THERAPIST UNDERGOES extensive training and practice to master a variety of massage techniques. However, such extensive training is not required for a parent to perform a good massage on a child.

I have written this chapter for parents. Chinese pediatric massage has numerous techniques, both basic and complex. The techniques I describe are the most simple and basic within the repertoire of CPM. Parents familiar with basic adult massage techniques will notice that some of the hand movements are similar to those used in other types of massage. Other techniques are unique, however, and require some practice to do well.

Much can be accomplished by the proficient use of several basic techniques. It is more important to perform several basic techniques well than to learn a large number of different ones.

TOUCH

Massage is about touch. The quality of touch, depth of pressure, and overall gentleness of the technique are important considerations. Remember that children's energy is easily accessible, and massage does not require heavy pressure to be effective. With adults you may need to use pressure to achieve the desired results; that is not the case with children.

While it is difficult to describe the proper degree of touch in words, a general guideline is to limit your pressure to the skin level. Do not try to press deeply into the muscles. With light pressure, you will be able to perform the movement of the technique very quickly and briskly. *Light, quick,* and *brisk* are the key words when you are performing these techniques. Books and videos can be useful aids in this learning process; however, seek feedback whenever possible from a trained practitioner.

TECHNIQUE QUALITIES

The four requirements for good technique are duration, force, gentleness, and rhythm (evenness). These qualities are necessary to produce the desired effect during the massage.

Duration: The technique must be performed for a long enough time to achieve the desired effect. Performing a motion well for only one minute when two minutes are required will not produce consistent results.

Force: The technique must achieve enough power to deal with the energetic condition of the child. Force does not mean pressure or physical strength. The force of a technique is the energetic power that results from the appropriate hand motion.

Gentleness: The technique should not create any more pain than the child is already experiencing. Each technique should be performed in a manner that is effective, yet also takes into account the child's tolerance level.

Rhythm (evenness): This is the smooth, regular, continuous pattern of applying the technique to the point. Of the four requirements, rhythm may be the most difficult to achieve. Each technique has its own rhythm. It is a very subjective quality, difficult to describe through words. However, rhythm is very comfortable and smooth when it is there and very conspicuous by its absence.

It may be difficult to learn techniques from a book. I present the information here as a reference to parents. If at all possible, seek guidance and feedback from a trained practitioner.

TONIFICATION AND CLEARING

The energetic effect of a technique can be described as either tonifying or clearing. Tonification is used to supplement a deficiency. It is used to strengthen an aspect that is weak. Clearing is used to decrease an excessive or stagnant energetic condition. This is an important distinction, because mistakenly applying an inappropriate technique could worsen the condition. For example, if a tonifying technique is applied to an excess condition it would add energy to an already overfull condition.

You can achieve tonification and clearing through your choice of technique and quality of manipulation. The techniques listed in this chapter can be categorized as primarily tonifying or clearing.

TECHNIQUE EFFECTS	
TONIFYING	CLEARING
Press	Push
Press Rotate	Push Apart
Rotate Push	Grasp
Spinal Pinch Pull	Fingernail Press
Rub Palms Together	

The action of the technique can also be influenced by the quality of movement you use. The qualities of tonifying techniques include light force, slow speed, and long duration. The qualities of clearing include strong force, quick speed, and short duration. For example, if you perform Rotate Push (see page 41) with light force, slowly, and for a long time, the effect will be tonifying. However, Rotate Push can also be performed with strong force, quickly, and for a short duration to make it clearing.

Rotate Push is very useful when working on the abdomen. When a deficient condition exists in the abdomen, using Rotate Push as a tonifying technique is appropriate. When an excessive condition exists in the abdomen, using Rotate Push as a clearing technique is appropriate.

The energetic action of the technique can also be influenced by the action of the point. Most points can be either tonified or cleared; however, some points are primarily used for one or the other effect. For example, *Three Passes* is a very strong tonifying point. Many of the massage plans use Push *Three Passes* as a primary tonification point. Even though Push is primarily a clearing technique, when it is combined with *Three Passes* the overall effect is tonifying.

NOTE

You need not understand all the details of tonifying and clearing techniques to perform an effective massage. Many of the decisions on which technique to use are made for you if you follow the steps of the massage plans. By identifying the energetic pattern (using the assessment skills and descriptions listed in each massage plan) and then using the techniques and points listed under that pattern, you will be treating with the appropriate techniques and points.

For example, the base plan for diarrhea is primarily composed of Press Rotate techniques, which are tonifying. Under the variations, the cold/damp pattern adds more tonifying techniques (Rub Palms Together and Press Rotate) to increase the tonifying aspects for a cold, deficient condition. The heat pattern adds clearing techniques (Push) to move the heat from the intestines.

LEARNING HOW TO PERFORM TECHNIQUES

The traditional way to learn techniques is to practice the movements on a rice bag, a small cloth bag or pillow filled with rice. With the proper amount of rice, this closely simulates the feel of working on a human body. It also provides a good context to learn the movements before using the technique on a child.

There is no exact size requirement for a rice bag. It should be large enough to allow full use of your hand to practice. An average-size bag measures 8 inches by 6 inches with approximately 3 inches of depth. The depth and density of the bag will be determined by how much rice you add—ideally, enough to form a dense, compact center that will allow a slight depression when you apply hand pressure. Too much rice will result in a bag that is too hard and has no give with pressure. Too little rice results in a bag that has no stable form, because the rice constantly shifts with pressure. The average-size bag described above contains approximately 3 pounds of rice (see figure 5).

Making a rice bag is fairly easy. Sew a small bag in the dimensions noted above, leaving a corner open. Fill the bag with rice and finish by closing the opening. Use a heavy-gauge thread and make the stitching strong. The bag should be sturdy, because it will need to endure repetitive motion and pressure. You can use almost any material; however, coarser and synthetic materials may be slightly irritating to the hand due to the repetitive nature of the techniques. It is also possible to sew a "pillowcase" to fit over the rice bag, which lets you use a softer material and wash the outer case when necessary.

A simpler way to create a rice bag is to buy a package of rice (usually 1 or 2 pounds in a plastic bag). Hold one end of the plastic bag and fold over any excess, securing

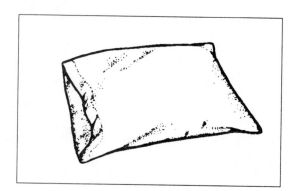

FIG. 5: RICE BAG

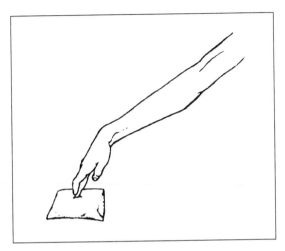

FIG. 6: ARM ANGLE TO RICE BAG

it with one or two pieces of tape. This will create a firmer working surface. Place the plastic rice bag in a pillowcase and fold the case over until it is neatly wrapped around the rice bag.

Practicing on the rice bag is fairly simple. Find a table of an appropriate height to work on. Stand at the side of the table with the rice bag directly in front of you. The ideal height of the table depends on your height. In the standing position your arms should be relaxed and have a natural downward angle toward the bag (see figure 6). If the table is too high your forearm will be parallel to the ground; if it is too low your arm will hang straight down, perpendicular to the ground. Both extremes make it difficult to practice the techniques. You can raise the height of the rice bag by inserting thin books under it until its position is ideal.

Using the descriptions of the techniques in this chapter, approach the rice bag as if it were a child, applying the technique to the "point." At first the movements may feel awkward and unnatural. This is why you practice on a rice bag and not on a child. Work out the awkwardness on the bag so that the technique is correct when you massage a child.

Some people may resist the process of practicing techniques on a rice bag. It does take time, patience, endurance, and attention to detail, but you will see the rewards for your effort when you successfully use massage on your child.

Technique Descriptions
氣

Press Techniques

This group of techniques involves the application of simple pressure held stationary on the selected point.

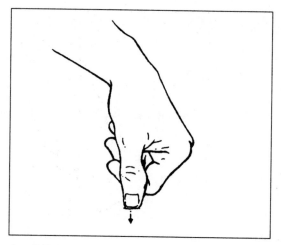

FIG. 7: PRESS

PRESS

Technique: Use your thumb, middle finger, or palm to press the point (see figure 7). Gradually increase the pressure from light to heavy. The depth and force depend on the condition. After forceful pressure, follow with Press Rotate. The movement of the Press technique is similar to pressing a button.

Action: Warm meridians, tranquilize mind, relieve pain.

PRESS ROTATE

Technique: This technique starts with Press and then adds a rotary movement with the part of the hand described below. Move your hand and wrist from your elbow in a relaxed, rhythmic, and swaying motion. The part of your hand in contact with the point should remain stationary. Your forearm describes a tight spiraling motion that travels down to the point in a funnel-like shape. The movement should be even, soft, and rhythmic; bring the skin along with the movement of your hand. The movement of Press Rotate is similar to using a pencil to fill in a small circle.

Action: Drive qi, activate blood, clear meridians, open organ obstructions.

With fingers (1, 2, 3): Using one, two, or three fingers (depending on the point), begin with Press and gradually begin the Press Rotate rotary motion, focusing on the fingertips or pads (see figures 8, 9, 10).

With palm edge: Use your greater thenar eminence (the large pad of the palm, just below the base of the thumb) as your only point

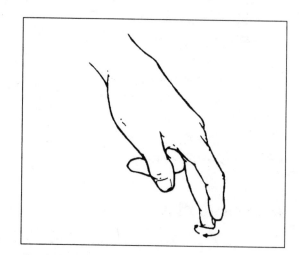

FIG. 8: PRESS ROTATE: 1 FINGER

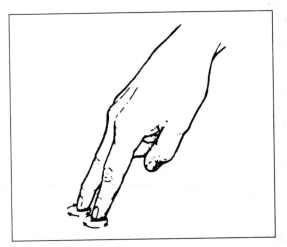

FIG. 9: PRESS ROTATE: 2 FINGERS

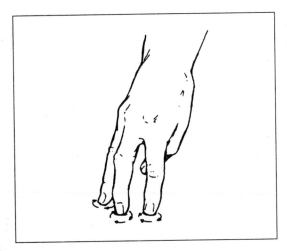

FIG. 10: PRESS ROTATE: 3 FINGERS

of contact with the child's point. Your hand and wrist will be slightly angled to achieve this position (see figure 11). The rotary motion mainly comes from a loose, flexible wrist.

With lower palm: Use the center of the lowest aspect of your palm (see figure 12). This requires less wrist action and more movement from your forearm and shoulder.

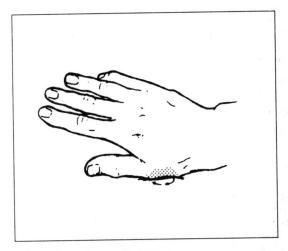

FIG. 11: PRESS ROTATE: PALM EDGE

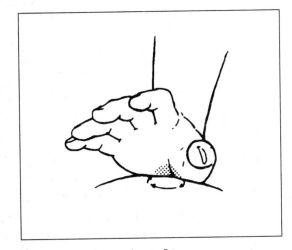

FIG. 12: PRESS ROTATE: LOWER PALM

FINGERNAIL PRESS

Technique: Use a thumbnail to apply force gradually and penetratingly (see figure 13). Do not cut the skin. Afterward, apply Press Rotate to relieve pain. The movement is similar to the Press technique.

Action: Calm fright, sober mind, open orifices, quell spasm, relieve twitch.

Push Techniques

In the Push techniques you will use your individual fingers or some combination of your thumb, index, middle fingers, and edge of the palm to push forcefully in a specific direction relative to the point. Use massage medium as needed. Your technique should be light and rapid, but it should not irritate the skin.

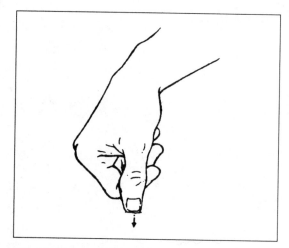

FIG. 13: FINGERNAIL PRESS

PUSH

Technique: The Push technique moves one-directionally in a linear fashion along the intended point (line) to avoid other points or meridians (see figures 14, 15). The movement of Push is similar to running your finger along a folded paper to form a crease.

Action: Relax tendons, activate blood, clear meridians, relieve pain.

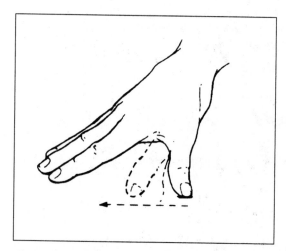

FIG. 14: PUSH: THUMB

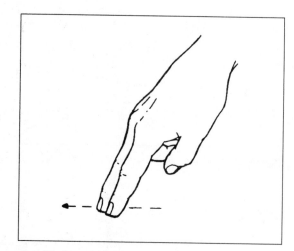

FIG. 15: PUSH: INDEX FINGER

PUSH APART

Technique: Using the tip of both thumb pads or your greater thenar eminence, push from the center of the point, moving both hands simultaneously away toward the periphery (see figure 16). The movement is one-directional and rapid with light pressure. The size and region of the point will determine the specifics of your motion. Push Apart mimics the movement of car windshield wipers, but only in the outward direction.

Action: Regulate and harmonize yin and yang, drive qi, activate blood, separate clear from turbid, drain turbid.

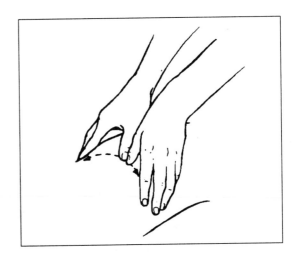

FIG. 16: PUSH APART

ROTATE PUSH

Technique: This technique is similar to Press Rotate except that the contact point of your hand does not stay stationary; instead it moves along the skin surface. Depending on the selected point, rotate in a circular motion according to the size of the point and the condition. Your fingers and hand should be relaxed and conform to the shape of the body area. A flexible and loose wrist is important to maintain a smooth, rhythmic motion. Rotate Push is similar to the circular movement used to wash large windows or mirrors.

Action: Regulate qi, harmonize blood.

With index and middle fingers: Use the pads of your index and middle fingers to rotate in a circular motion over a small point area (see figure 17).

With index, middle, and ring fingers: Use the pads of these fingers to rotate in a circular

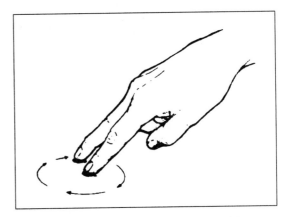

FIG. 17: ROTATE PUSH: INDEX AND MIDDLE FINGERS

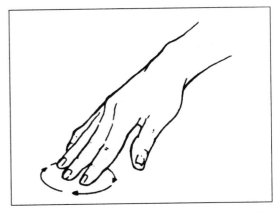

FIG. 18: ROTATE PUSH: INDEX, MIDDLE, AND RING FINGERS

motion over the point area (see figure 18).

SPINAL PINCH PULL

Technique: Begin at the sacrum with one hand on each side of the spine. Grip the skin with both of your thumbs and index fingers. Gently lift up and begin moving along the spine, continuously rolling the skin up and lifting it away from the spine (see figure 19). Continue along the length of

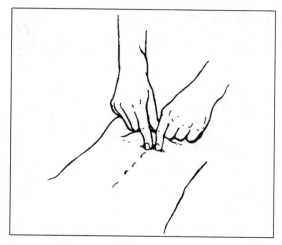

FIG. 19: SPINAL PINCH PULL

the spine to the base of the neck. This technique is only used in one direction, from the lower back to the upper back. The movement is quick and light—you take only one to two seconds to go from lower to upper back. Spinal Pinch Pull is somewhat similar to evening out a bulge in a carpet by pushing it toward the edge.

Action: Regulate yin, yang, qi, and blood; harmonize organs, promote smooth meridian function, tonify deficiency.

GRASPING

Technique: Using your thumb and index finger, gently grip the skin on the point, lifting quickly and repeatedly until the point begins to color. Grasping is somewhat similar to the movement used to pluck out small weeds or blades of grass from the garden.

Action: Induce perspiration, relieve exterior, clear orifices, sober mind, regulate and harmonize qi and blood.

RUB PALMS TOGETHER

Technique: Briskly rub your palms together, using little pressure but rapid, repetitive back-and-forth motions. After generating significant heat (qi), approximately 15 to 20 seconds, cover the point. Rub Palms Together is similar to the movement used to warm your hands during cold weather.

Action: Tonify deficiency, warm meridians, nourish original yang.

4
POINT LOCATIONS

IN PEDIATRIC MASSAGE THE FOCUS OF THE TECHNIQUES is on a point. In general, the definition of a *point* is "a place where qi gathers and can be influenced." A majority of the information on points comes from the field of acupuncture, in which practitioners insert very small needles into points—thus their focus on points as small dots. Because many Oriental massage styles have adopted the acupuncture point numbering system, most people familiar with Oriental massage conceive of a point as a dot. For the purposes of pediatric massage, however, points are better defined as areas than as small dots. Indeed, some pediatric points are lines, such as *Three Passes*—a line that extends from the wrist to the elbow crease on the inner forearm. Other pediatric points are larger body areas, such as *Scapula*—the area on the back between the shoulder blades.

One explanation for this difference in pediatric points is that a child's energetic system is immature; it has not yet fully evolved into the complete system of points and meridians found in adults. In this way children's points may be more compact or different from adults'.

For example, in an adult the lung meridian extends from the thumb along the arm up to the side of the chest on both arms (see figure 20). This meridian has eleven points. A massage therapist or acupuncturist chooses from the different energetic functions of the eleven points to influence the lungs.

On children the lung meridian is represented by the

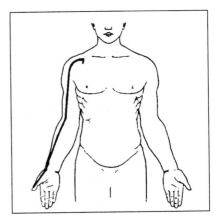

FIG. 20: ADULT LUNG MERIDIAN

area of the tip of the fourth finger on both hands (see figure 21). To influence the lungs we choose a technique to tonify the lungs (Press Rotate) if they are deficient, or one to clear the lungs (Push) if they are excessive.

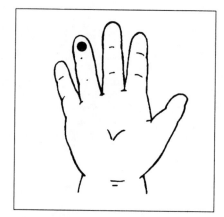

FIG. 21: CHILD LUNG MERIDIAN

Over the centuries, Chinese pediatricians have collected and categorized a distinct set of pediatric points based on their practical experience. Some pediatric points are similar to adult points, but others are unique to children. In some instances the point name and location are similar in children and adults; however, the energetic function may differ.

Pediatric points have never been Westernized by substituting a number for the Chinese name as has occurred in acupuncture. For example, the Chinese name for an influential point on the hand is He gu. To simplify learning for non-Chinese students it is called *Large Intestine 4*, because it is the fourth point from the beginning of the large intestine meridian. Many Western-trained acupuncturists and massage therapists know these points only by the numbering system.

In this book English translations of the Chinese names are used because they give an indication of the *character* of the point, which is generally reflected in its name. While this may seem cumbersome to learn, the name of the point is usually a description of the location or function of the point. An example is the point *Abdominal Corner*, whose name gives a good description of its location. The point *Welcome Fragrance* is located on either side of the nostrils and used to open up a stuffy nose, hence the name.

In this chapter I will present 63 points, from a total of 170 points generally used in Chinese pediatric massage. You need not memorize all 63 points. In fact, you can treat most conditions with a basic understanding of 20 to 25 points. You can learn points as the need arises, although it is best to take some time beforehand to get a general sense of all of them. For example, you may become very comfortable with the 10 points in the General Health Care massage plan. If your child develops a cold, then you will learn three to five points beyond what you already know. The information for each point presents some indications that are not covered by the massage plans. These represent instances in which it is likely that you would have already consulted your family practitioner.

In this chapter the points are organized by body region, along with illustrations for each region and each individual point. Regional illustrations are included to show the relationship between points in close proximity. Numbers following the point names are provided to help you locate the point only on the regional illustration.

The information on each individual point includes its location, technique, action, and indications for usage. In addition, the Chinese name in pinyin and, where relevant, the acupuncture point number (in parentheses) are given.

NOTE

To help you locate points, some of the descriptions use the finger width of the child being massaged as a standard measurement. This helps you adjust for variations in body size. For example, the location of *Elixir Field* is defined as three of the child's finger widths below the navel. You can place the child's hand at the location to measure. You can also measure how many of your own fingers equal three of the child's, then use your own fingers to measure.

Hand Region

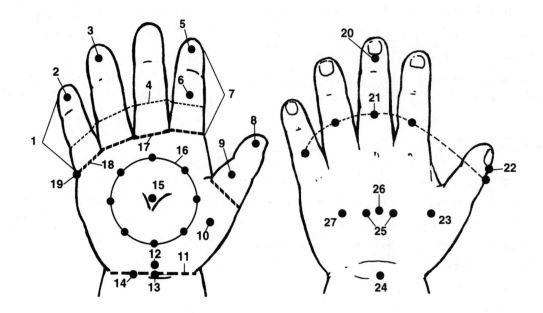

HAND POINT NAMES

Chief Tendon (13)

External Palace of Labor (26)

Five Digital Joints (21)

Four Transverse Lines (4)

Gallbladder Meridian (6)

Inner Eight Symbols (16)

Inner Palace of Labor (15)

Kidney Line (18)

Kidney Meridian (2)

Large Intestine Meridian (7)

Large Transverse Line (11)

Liver Meridian (5)

Lung Meridian (3)

Maternal Cheek (22)

Old Dragon (20)

One Nestful Wind (24)

Palmar Small Transverse Line (19)

Small Celestial Center (12)

Small Intestine Meridian (1)

Small Transverse Lines (17)

Spleen Meridian (8)

Stomach Meridian (9)

Two Horses (27)

Two Leaf Doors (25)

Union Valley (23)

White Tendon (14)

Wood Gate (10)

CHIEF TENDON   ZHONG JIN

Location: Midpoint on the inner wrist crease.

Technique: Press Rotate 100–300 times *or* Fingernail Press 3–5 times.

Action: Disperse heat, relieve spasms, ease mind, calm fright, reduce fever, disperse stagnation.

Indications: Convulsions, mental stress, diarrhea, vomiting, mouth ulcers, night crying, fever, toothache.

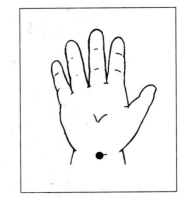

EXTERNAL PALACE OF LABOR   WAI LAO GONG

Location: Center of the back of the hand (opposite *Inner Palace of Labor*)

Technique: Rotate Push 100–200 times *or* Fingernail Press 3–5 times then Rotate Press 100–300 times.

Action: Warm yang qi, disperse pathological cold, consolidate and warm lower abdomen, disperse external heat, promote digestion, remove stagnation, relieve pain.

Indications: Stool with undigested food, intestinal gurgling, diarrhea, dysentery (cold), abdominal pain, hernia, prolapsed anus, intestinal parasites, external diseases, bed-wetting, abdominal distension, hot body, headache.

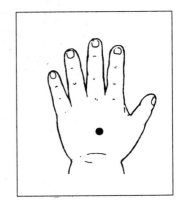

FIVE DIGITAL JOINTS   WU ZHI JIE

Location: Back of the hand, middle joint on each of the five fingers.

Technique: Press 3–5 times *or* Press Rotate 100–200 times *or* Fingernail Press 3–5 times then Press Rotate 100–300 times.

Action: Resuscitate unconsciousness, stop convulsions, open orifices, resolve phlegm, disperse cold and heat, disperse external pathogens.

Indications: Convulsions, spasms, coma, cough, runny nose, poor appetite, external symptoms.

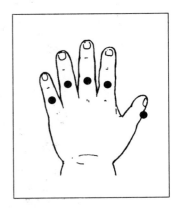

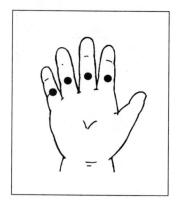

FOUR TRANSVERSE LINES   SUI WEN

Location: Palm of the hand, lines at the second segment of all four fingers.

Technique: Fingernail Press 3 times then Press Rotate 30–50 times *or* Push back and forth 300–400 times.

Action: Relieve chest, facilitate diaphragm movement, promote digestion, resolve phlegm.

Indications: Abdominal distension, chest congestion and oppression, labored breathing, productive cough, chapped lips, abdominal pain, poor appetite.

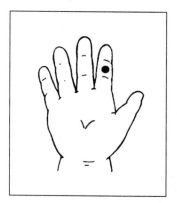

GALLBLADDER MERIDIAN   DAN JING   (GB)

Location: Index finger, palm side of the second segment.

Technique: *Clear:* Push from the end closest to the fingertip toward the palm 100–500 times. *Tonify:* Press Rotate 100–500 times.

Action: Pacify and relax gallbladder, disperse gallbladder heat.

Indications: Earache, gallbladder meridian inflammations.

INNER EIGHT SYMBOLS   NEI BA GUA

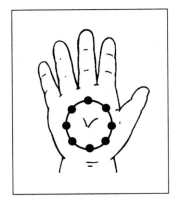

Location: A circle around the midpoint of the palm (*Inner Palace of Labor*).

The *Inner Eight Symbols* refer to the Chinese Ba Gua. The eight symbols each refer to a particular element within nature that can be manipulated for a specific effect.

For those familiar with the I Ching, or the Ba Gua, the element locations can be described using the analogy of a clock face. Look at the left palm and imagine the *Inner Eight Symbol* circle there. At the junction of the third finger and the palm is 12 o'clock. Sky (Qian) is at 4 o'clock; Water (Kan) at 6 o'clock; Mountain (Gen) at 8 o'clock; Thunder (Zhen) at 9 o'clock; Wind (Xun) at 10 o'clock; Fire (Li) at 12 o'clock; Earth (Kun) at 2 o'clock; and Ocean (Dui) at 3 o'clock.

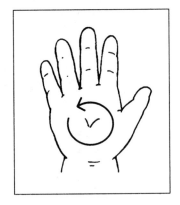

Technique: Rotate Push 100–500 times.

The direction of rotation around *Inner Eight Symbols* is important. There are two directions of movement: normal flow and counterflow. In normal flow move clockwise around the child's left hand, counterclockwise around the right hand. In counterflow move counterclockwise around the child's left hand; clockwise around the right hand.

The action of normal flow is to raise qi, meaning to move it upward in the body. This is the typical tonifying action for children. However, some conditions are already moving upward in the body and would be aggravated by more upward movement. For example, coughing and vomiting are characterized by upward movement. For these types of conditions you should thus push *Inner Eight Symbols* in the counterflow direction. The action of counterflow is to descend qi in the body. When "Rotate Push *Inner Eight Symbols*" is listed in a massage plan, it signifies using normal flow. When counterflow is needed, this is indicated next to Rotate Push *Inner Eight Symbols* in the list of techniques and points (for example, see the Cough massage plan on pages 94–95).

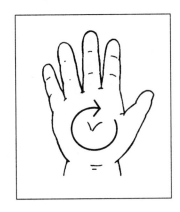

Action: Regulate and remove obstruction of qi and blood, harmonize yin organs, relieve chest, resolve phlegm, facilitate diaphragm movement, promote digestion, depress adverse rising stomach qi.

Normal flow: Raise qi.

Counterflow: Descend qi.

Indications: Cough, diarrhea, abdominal distension, food stagnancy, vomiting, labored breathing (phlegm), dyspepsia, loss of appetite, chest oppression, vexation, restlessness.

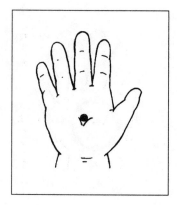

INNER PALACE OF LABOR   NEI LAO GONG   (P 8)

Location: Center of the palm; a flexed middle finger will touch the point.

Technique: Press Rotate 50–300 times *or* Rotate Push 30–100 times.

Action: Clear heat, relieve exterior symptoms, stop convulsions.

Indications: Fright, convulsions, common-cold fever, excess heat patterns, deficient heat patterns, heart fever, vexation, internal heat, thrush, gum erosion, high fever, twitching.

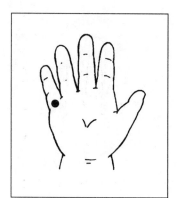

KIDNEY LINE   SHEN WEN

Location: Root of the little finger, crease at the palm.

Technique: Press Rotate 100–500 times *or* Press 100–300 times.

Action: Expel wind, brighten eyes, disperse lumps and stagnation, clear stagnant heat, lead fire outward.

Indications: Red eyes, thrush, toxic heat patterns, conjunctivitis, internal heat with external cold.

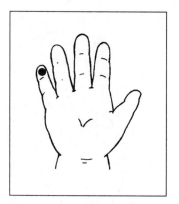

KIDNEY MERIDIAN   SHEN JING   (K)

Location: Little fingertip pad.

Technique: *Tonify:* Press Rotate 100–500 times. *Clear:* Push tip toward palm.

Action: *Tonify:* Strengthen kidneys and yang qi. *Clear:* Purge stagnant heat in lower abdomen.

Indications: Congenital deficiencies, postillness weakness, morning diarrhea, bed-wetting, cough, asthma, frequent or difficult urination, convulsions, epilepsy, toothache, paralysis aftermath.

LARGE INTESTINE MERIDIAN   DA CHANG JING   (LI)

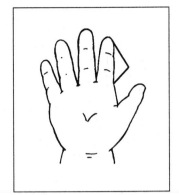

Location: Edge of the index finger that faces the thumb, from the tip to the web.

Technique: *Tonify:* Push from the tip to the web 100–500 times. *Clear:* Push from the web to the tip 100–500 times.

Action: *Tonify:* Regulate intestinal function. *Clear:* Clear large intestine heat, relax bowels.

Indications: Diarrhea, dysentery, constipation, abdominal pain, anal swelling and redness.

LARGE TRANSVERSE LINE   DA HENG WEN

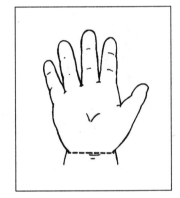

Location: Palm side of the wrist crease.

Technique: 1. Press Rotate 100–500 times. 2. Push Apart 80–300 times.

Action: 1. Expel wind, depress adverse rising qi, balance yin yang, remove food stagnation. 2. Balance yin yang, harmonize and regulate yin organs.

Indications: 1. Vomiting, alternating chills and fever, asthma with sputum, food stagnation, abdominal distension, diarrhea. 2. Convulsions, epilepsy, coma, twitching, food retention, diarrhea, dysentery.

LIVER MERIDIAN   GAN JING   (LV)

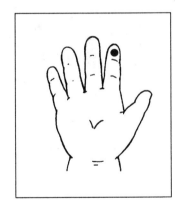

Location: Index fingertip pad.

Technique: Push from the side closest to the palm toward the tip 100–500 times *or* Push back and forth 100–300 times. *Note:* It is uncommon to tonify *Liver Meridian.* If necessary, this can be accomplished by tonifying *Kidney Meridian.* An exception may be when treating mumps.

Action: Clear liver and gallbladder heat, ease mind, relieve convulsions, settle liver, expel wind, reduce fever.

Indications: Convulsions, red eyes, anxiety, restlessness, fright, irritability, hot soles or palms, sore throat, conjunctivitis, twitching with high fever, thrush, urination difficulties, deep-colored urine, diarrhea, abdominal distension.

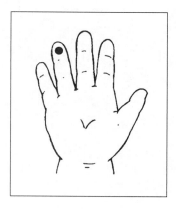

LUNG MERIDIAN   FEI JING

Location: Fourth (ring) fingertip pad.

Technique: *Clear:* Push the tip toward the palm 100–500 times. *Tonify:* Press Rotate 100–500 times.

Action: Clear throat, stop cough, smooth qi, resolve phlegm, relax bowels. *Tonify:* Strengthen lungs. *Clear:* Expel excess lung heat.

Indications: Common cold, cough, asthma with sputum, constipation, fever, stuffy chest, labored breathing (phlegm), dry throat.

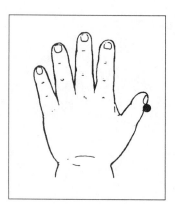

MATERNAL CHEEK   MU SAI

Location: Just below the thumbnail at the midpoint of the nail's width.

Technique: Fingernail Press 3–5 times.

Action: Stop bleeding and vomiting.

Indications: Bleeding, vomiting.

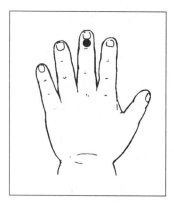

OLD DRAGON   LAO LONG

Location: Just below the middle fingernail at the midpoint of the nail's width.

Technique: Fingernail Press 3–10 times.

Action: Resuscitate unconsciousness, stop convulsions, reduce fever and pathological fire, open orifices, recuperate yang.

Indications: Acute febrile convulsions, fever, irritability, fright, restlessness, afternoon fever, dull mind, wailing, coma.

ONE NESTFUL WIND   YI WO FENG

Location: Back of the hand at the midpoint on the wrist crease.

Technique: Press Rotate 100–300 times *or* Fingernail Press 10–20 times *or* Push Apart 50–100 times (less intense than Fingernail Press).

Action: Warm abdomen, increase qi circulation, relieve abdominal pain, relieve joint pain, expel wind or cold, calm fright, ease mind, relieve pain, relieve external symptoms.

Indications: Abdominal pain, intestinal gurgling, common cold, swelling and painful joints, convulsions.

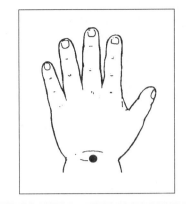

PALMAR SMALL TRANSVERSE LINE   ZHENG XIAO HENG WEN

Location: Base of the little finger on the palm side, outside edge of the crease.

Technique: Press Rotate 100–300 times *or* Push back and forth 100–300 times.

Action: Clear heat, disperse stagnation, ventilate lungs, resolve cough and phlegm.

Indications: Labored breathing (phlegm), cough, fever, thrush.

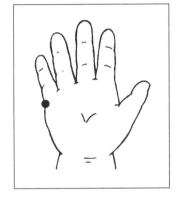

SMALL CELESTIAL CENTER   XIAO TIAN XIN

Location: Base of the palm at the midpoint, just above the wrist crease.

Technique: Press Rotate 100–300 times *or* Fingernail Press 3–5 times.

Action: Clear orifices, eliminate stagnation, stop convulsions, ease mind, brighten eyes, clear pathogenic heat, promote urination, calm fright.

Indications: Convulsions, epilepsy, blurred vision, eye redness, eye pain and swelling, excess tears, unclosed fontanel, high fever, coma, vexation, restlessness, night crying, insomnia, reduced urination, incomplete measles or pox.

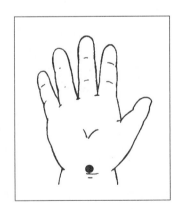

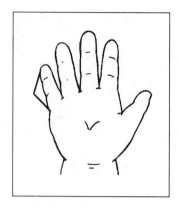

SMALL INTESTINE MERIDIAN   XIAO CHANG JING

Location: Outside edge of the little finger from the tip to the root.

Technique: *Clear:* Push base to tip 100–500 times.

Action: Clear heat, promote urination.

Indications: Diarrhea, scant urine, high fever, afternoon fever, bed-wetting, dark urine, thrush.

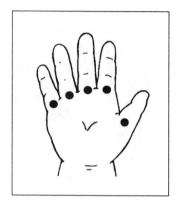

SMALL TRANSVERSE LINES   SUI HENG WEN

Location: All five fingers at the palm-side creases where the fingers join the palm.

Technique: Fingernail Press 2–5 times *or* Push back and forth 50–100 times *or* Press Rotate 100–300 times.

Action: Clear heat, eliminate vexation, disperse stagnation, resolve phlegm.

Indications: Fever, fretfulness, thrush, cough, labored breathing.

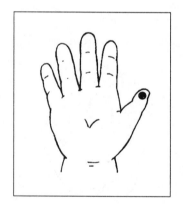

SPLEEN MERIDIAN   PI JING   (SP)

Location: Thumbtip pad.

Technique: *Tonify:* Press Rotate 300–500 times. *Clear:* Push from the palm from the side to the tip 300–500 times.

Action: *Tonify:* Strengthen stomach and spleen, nourish blood, resolve phlegm. *Clear:* Remove food stagnation, promote digestion, eliminate dampness.

Indications: Spleen and stomach deficiency, loss of appetite, emaciation, listlessness, diarrhea, indigestion, constipation, poor appetite, dysentery, convulsions, damp, phlegm, jaundice, abdominal distension, spontaneous sweating, night sweats, muscle atrophy, incomplete measles or pox.

STOMACH MERIDIAN   WEI JING   (ST)

Location: Thumb, second segment of palm side, outer edge.

Technique: *Tonify:* Press Rotate 300–500 times. *Clear:* Push from the palm side toward the tip 300–500 times.

Action: Stop vomiting, promote digestion, clear heat.

Indications: Vomiting, hiccough, thirst, poor appetite, pathologic stomach fire, abdominal distension, loss of appetite, diarrhea.

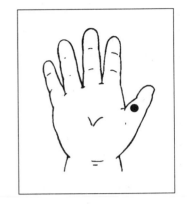

TWO HORSES   ER MA

Location: Back of the hand, toward the little-finger side of the center between the fourth and fifth finger bones.

Technique: Press Rotate 100–300 times *or* Fingernail Press 5–10 times.

Action: Tonify kidneys, retrieve yang, lead fire to original place, drive qi, disperse stagnation.

Indications: Urination difficulties, indigestion, abdominal pain, weak constitution, prolapsed rectum, bed-wetting, cough, asthma, dark urine, toothache, phlegm, dampness, teeth grinding, coma, lumbago, tinnitus, leg flaccidity, neck swelling or pain.

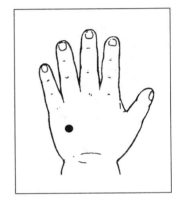

TWO LEAF DOORS   ER SHAN MEN

Location: On the back of the hand, the two depressions on either side of the center.

Technique: Press both points 3–5 times *or* Press Rotate 300–500 times.

Action: Relieve exterior, promote smooth circulation of qi and blood to relax muscles and tendons, expel wind, relieve labored breathing.

Indications: Febrile symptoms due to pathogenic wind or cold, asthma with sputum, stuffy chest, convulsions, febrile with no sweating, common cold, labored breathing (phlegm), cough, incomplete measles or pox.

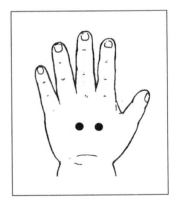

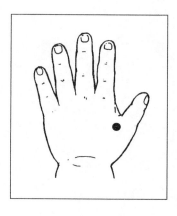

UNION VALLEY   HE GU   (LI 4)

Location: On the back of the hand, the end of the thumb-side crease in the web between the thumb and index finger.

Technique: Press Rotate 100–200 times *or* Fingernail Press 3–5 times then Press Rotate 50–100 times.

Action: Induce perspiration, relieve exterior, remove stagnation, clear heat, relieve pain.

Indications: Headache, stiff neck, fever without perspiration, sore throat, toothache, constipation, vomiting.

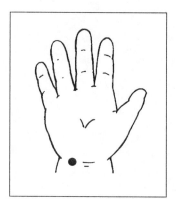

WHITE TENDON   BAI JIN

Location: Palm-side wrist crease midway between the midpoint and the little-finger side of the wrist.

Technique: Fingernail Press 3–5 times *or* Press Rotate 50–100 times.

Action: Smooth qi flow, resolve phlegm, relieve chest, facilitate diaphragm.

Indications: Chest oppression, labored breathing (phlegm).

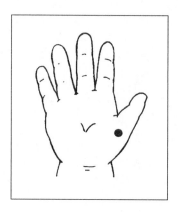

WOOD GATE   BAN MEN

Location: Center of the fleshy part of the palm directly beneath the thumb (greater thenar eminence).

Technique: *Tonify:* Press Rotate 100–300 times. *Clear:* Push 100–200 times.

Action: Relieve convulsions, remove food stagnancy, promote digestion, drain excess heat of stomach and spleen, tonify spleen/harmonize stomach, cool diaphragm.

Indications: Acute/chronic convulsions, indigestion, vomiting, diarrhea, shortness of breath.

Arm Region

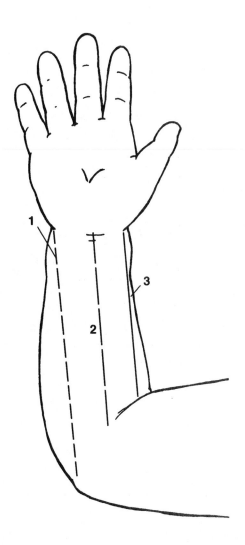
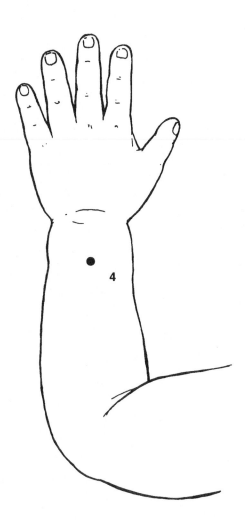

ARM POINT NAMES

Arm Yang Pool (4)

Six Hollow Bowels (1)

Three Passes (3)

Water of Galaxy (2)

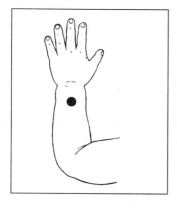

Arm Yang Pool   Bo yang qi

Location: On the back of the hand, three of the child's finger widths above the wrist crease *(One Nestful Wind)*.

Technique: Press Rotate 300–500 times *or* Fingernail Press 5–7 times then Press Rotate 10–30 times.

Action: Lead fire downward, disperse heat.

Indications: Dizziness, headache, convulsions, epilepsy, constipation, urination difficulties, dark urine, dry stool, diarrhea, bed-wetting.

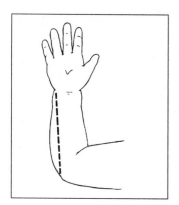

Six Hollow Bowels   Liu fu

Location: Lower edge of the ulnar bone on the forearm, from the elbow to the wrist crease.

Technique: Push from the elbow to the wrist 100–500 times.

Action: Clear heat, cool blood, detoxify, resolve swelling, relieve pain.

Indications: High fever, irritability, dry stools, thirst, desire for cold drinks, heat patterns, convulsions, thrush, swollen tongue, gum ulcer, throat pain, swelling, mumps, sores, stagnant accumulation in bowels, dysentery, constipation.

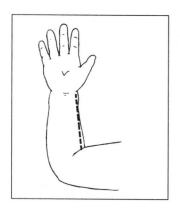

Three Passes   San guan

Location: Inner side of the forearm on the thumb side (radial bone border), from the wrist crease to the elbow joint.

Technique: Push from the wrist to the elbow 100–500 times (increase the number for cold patterns).

Action: Reinforce qi, tonify yang qi, disperse pathogenic cold, relieve exterior patterns, tonify deficiency, promote flow of qi, activate blood, cultivate and supplement kidney qi.

Indications: Abdominal pain, diarrhea, postillness weakness, cold aversion, weak limbs, loss of appetite, jaundice, anemia, incomplete measles or pox, polio, boils, spontaneous perspiration, deficient qi and blood, weak constitution, yang deficiency.

Note: Do not use with excess or heat patterns.

WATER OF GALAXY   TIAN HE SHUI

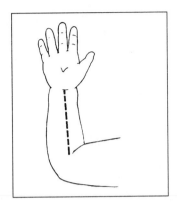

Location: Midline of the inside forearm, from the wrist crease to the elbow crease.

Technique: Push from the wrist to the elbow 100–500 times.

Action: Clear pathogenic heat, relieve exterior, clear pathogenic fire, eliminate vexation and fretfulness, calm fright, reduce excess patterns, clear heat patterns.

Indications: Fever and heat patterns, common-cold fever, tidal fever, excess internal heat, irritability, restlessness, thirst, stiff tongue, convulsions, fright crying, fretfulness, abdominal distension, stomach or spleen heat, thrush, swollen gums, cough, labored breathing (phlegm), dry stool, dark urine, excess and heat patterns.

Front Torso Region

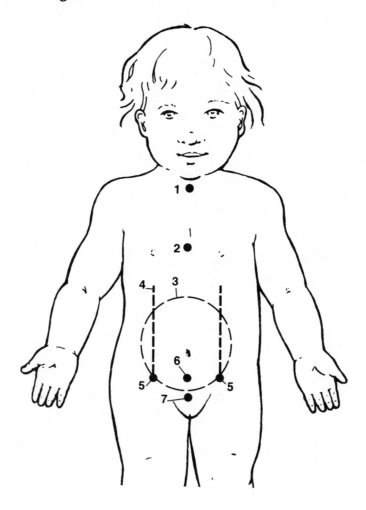

FRONT OF TORSO POINT NAMES

Abdomen (3)

Abdominal Corner (5)

Below Ribs (4)

Celestial Chimney (1)

Chest Center (2)

Curved Bone (7)

Elixir Field (6)

ABDOMEN   FU

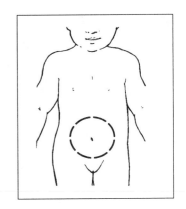

Location: Front of the torso, between the lowest ribs and the pubic bone.

Technique: Rotate Push 36 rotations clockwise then 36 counterclockwise. Repeat for 5–7 minutes *or* Push Apart from the midline to side 50–100 times.

Action: Promote digestion, warm yang qi, tonify stomach and spleen, regulate gastrointestinal functions, relieve indigestion, disperse stagnant qi, relieve abdominal pain and distension.

Indications: Abdominal pain, indigestion, vomiting, diarrhea, constipation, abdominal distension, intestinal gurgling, food retention, malnutrition.

ABDOMINAL CORNER   DU JIAO

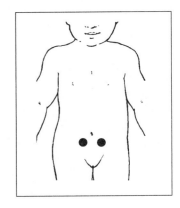

Location: From the navel, three of the child's finger widths outside and three of the child's finger widths below the navel, on both sides.

Technique: Grasp 3–5 times.

Action: Relieve abdominal pain due to pathogenic cold or irregular diet, disperse cold, clear heat, disperse stagnation, stop diarrhea, relax bowels.

Indications: Abdominal pain (especially pathogenic cold), diarrhea, constipation, dysentery.

BELOW RIBS   XIE LEI

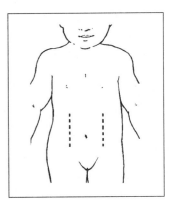

Location: Below the lowest rib at the midpoint between the sternum and the end of the rib, a line running down to *Abdominal Corner*.

Technique: Push from the ribs downward 100–300 times.

Action: Regulate qi flow, resolve phlegm, regulate large intestine, remove food stagnation, eliminate distension, promote digestion.

Indications: Indigestion, stuffy chest, abdominal distension (phlegm), stagnant food retention, abdominal pain, constipation, intestinal gurgling.

Note: Shift emphasis closer to the midline of the body for diarrhea.

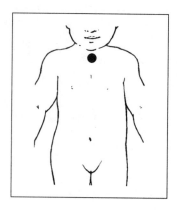

Celestial Chimney   Tian tu   (CV 22)

Location: Center of the bony notch at the base of the throat.

Technique: Press Rotate 30–50 times *or* Fingernail Press 3–5 times.

Action: Clear phlegm obstruction, clear heat, open throat, depress adverse rising qi, relieve labored breathing, stop vomiting.

Indications: Labored breathing, sore throat, hoarseness, insufficient phlegm discharge, cough, sudden vomiting.

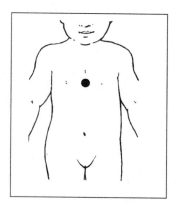

Chest Center   Dan zhong   (CV 17)

Location: Chest midline between the nipples.

Technique: Press Rotate 30–60 times *or* Push (downward) 50–100 times *or* Push Apart 50–100 times.

Action: Regulate lung qi, stop cough, relieve chest distress, smooth qi flow, relieve labored breathing.

Indications: Stuffy chest, asthma, cough, vomiting, nausea, labored breathing (phlegm), wheezing, diaphragm distension, hiccough, phlegm, bronchitis.

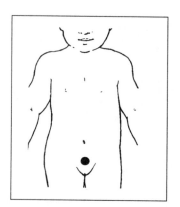

Curved Bone   Qu gu   (CV 2)

Location: Midpoint of the pubic bone at its upper border.

Technique: Press Rotate 200–500 times.

Action: Tonify kidneys, tonify lower abdomen.

Indications: Bed-wetting (enuresis).

ELIXIR FIELD   DAN TIAN

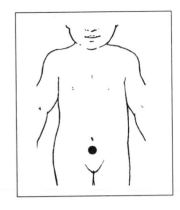

Location: Three of the child's finger widths directly below the navel.

Technique: Press Rotate 100–300 times *or* Rotate Push 30–50 times.

Action: Tonify kidneys.

Indications: Diarrhea, abdominal pain, bed-wetting, prolapsed rectum, hernia, urination difficulties, congenital qi deficiency.

Back of Torso Region

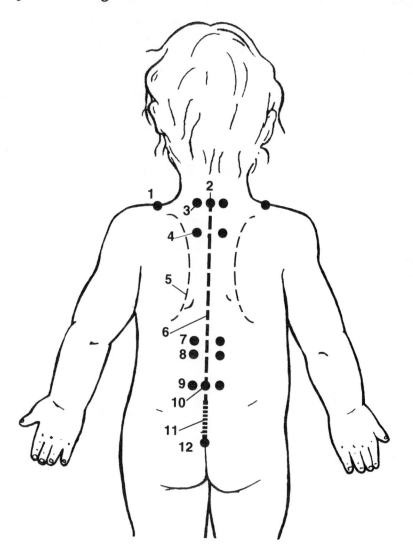

BACK OF TORSO POINT NAMES

Bone of Seven Segments (11)   Scapula (5)
Calm Breath (3)   Shoulder Well (1)
Great Hammer (2)   Spinal Column (6)
Kidney Back Point (9)   Spleen Back Point (7)
Life Gate (10)   Stomach Back Point (8)
Lung Back Point (4)   Tortoise Tail (12)

BONE OF SEVEN SEGMENTS   QI JIE GU

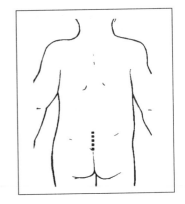

Location: On the spine, from L-2 (*Life Gate*) to the tailbone (*Tortoise Tail*).

Technique: Push 100–300 times *or* Rotate Push 100–200 times.

Action: Relax bowels, stop diarrhea, relieve constipation. *Push (down):* Relieve constipation. *Push (up):* Stop diarrhea.

Indications: Diarrhea, constipation, dysentery, prolapsed rectum. *Push (down):* Constipation. *Push (up):* Diarrhea.

CALM BREATH   DING CHUAN   (X 14)

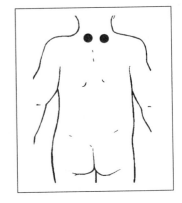

Location: Upper back on both sides of *Great Hammer*, approximately at the level of C-7 and T-1.

Technique: Press Rotate 100–300 times.

Action: Relieve cough, disperse stagnant lung qi, open lungs.

Indications: Asthma, cough, rubella.

GREAT HAMMER   DA ZHUI   (GV 14)

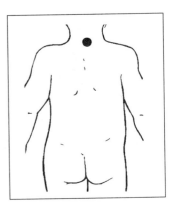

Location: Upper back midline at the base of the neck (between C-7 and T-1).

Technique: Press Rotate 50–100 times.

Action: Induce perspiration, relieve exterior, relieve labored breathing, stop vomiting, clear heat, expel wind, relax spasms, remove external attack, clear heart and lung heat.

Indications: External fever, stiff neck, labored breathing, vomiting, diarrhea, convulsions, common cold, shoulder pain.

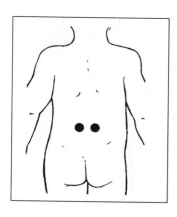

KIDNEY BACK POINT   SHEN SHU   (BL 23)

Location: Lower back, two of the child's finger widths on either side of *Life Gate* (directly opposite the navel at the level of L-2: see below).

Technique: Press Rotate 100–300 times.

Action: Tonify kidneys, warm yang qi.

Indications: Kidney deficiency, diarrhea, bed-wetting (enuresis), limb weakness.

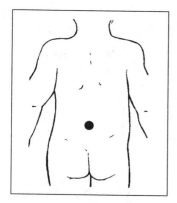

LIFE GATE   MING MEN   (GV 4)

Location: Lower back, on the spine, directly opposite the navel (below L-2 spinous process).

Technique: Press Rotate 100–300 times *or* Rub Palms Together and Press until warm.

Action: Tonify kidneys, warm yang qi, supplement and tonify essence.

Indications: Bed-wetting (enuresis), kidney deficiency or weakness.

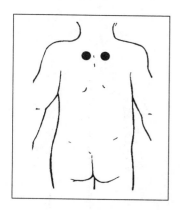

LUNG BACK POINT   FEI SHU   (BL 13)

Location: Upper back, two of the child's finger widths on each side of T-3, approximately at the level of the top of the shoulder blade.

Technique: Press Rotate 100–200 times *or* Push (down) along the scapula border 100–300 times *or* Push Apart 50–100 times.

Action: Clear lung heat, tonify deficiency, stop cough, relieve labored breathing, regulate lung qi.

Indications: Lung heat, labored breathing, accumulated heat in chest, common cold, cough, lung deficiency due to protracted cough.

SCAPULA   JIAN JIE GU

Location: The area between both shoulder blades.

Technique: Push Apart, moving from top to bottom and back again repeatedly, 100–300 times.

Action: Disperse excess lung qi, resolve cough, relieve asthma.

Indications: Lung qi dysfunction, cough, asthma.

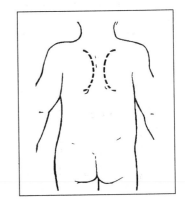

SHOULDER WELL   JIAN JING   **(GB 21)**

Location: Upper back, the midpoint between *Great Hammer* (C-7 and T-1) and the highest point on the shoulder.

Technique: Grasp 5–10 times *or* Press 5–10 times.

Action: Relax tendons and ligaments, improve qi and blood circulation.

Indications: Neck rigidity, shoulder and head conditions.

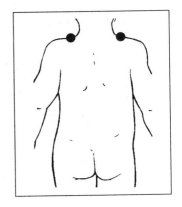

SPINAL COLUMN   JI ZHU

Location: Midline of the back, from the *Great Hammer* to *Tortoise Tail* (C-7 to tailbone: see page 68).

Technique: Push from above to below 300–500 times *or* Spinal Pinch Pull 3–5 times.

Action: Reduce fever, eliminate distension, tonify stomach and spleen, regulate yin-yang qi and blood, harmonize organs, promote smooth meridian function. Push (down): Clear excess. Spinal Pinch Pull: Tonify deficiency.

Indications: Fever, malnutrition, stomach or spleen deficiency, convulsions, night crying, diarrhea, vomiting, abdominal pain, constipation. *Push (down):* Fever, convulsions. *Spinal Pinch Pull:* Malnutrition, deficiency diarrhea.

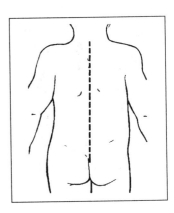

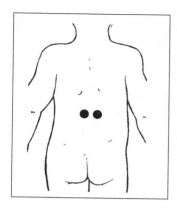

SPLEEN BACK POINT   PI SHU   (BL 20)

Location: Middle back, two of the child's finger widths on either side of the spine approximately at the level of the second-lowest rib (T-11).

Technique: Press Rotate 50–100 times.

Action: Tonify stomach and spleen, promote digestion, eliminate dampness, promote food assimilation.

Indications: Vomiting, malnutrition, convulsions, weak limbs, diarrhea, spleen deficiency.

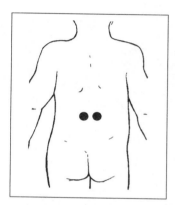

STOMACH BACK POINT   WEI SHU   (BL 21)

Location: Middle back, two of the child's finger widths on either side of spine approximately at the level of the lowest rib, T-12 (just below *Spleen Back Point*).

Technique: Press Rotate 50–100 times.

Action: Tonify stomach and spleen, promote digestion, eliminate dampness, clear stomach heat.

Indications: Digestive distress, vomiting.

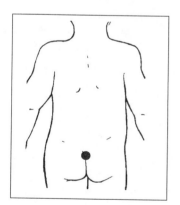

TORTOISE TAIL   GUI WEI   (GV 1)

Location: Just below the tailbone (coccyx tip).

Technique: Press Rotate 300–500 times *or* Fingernail Press 3–5 times then Press Rotate 30–50 times.

Action: Stop diarrhea, relax bowels, calm fright, warm yang qi.

Indications: Convulsions, constipation, diarrhea, abdominal pain, dysentery, prolapsed rectum.

Leg Region

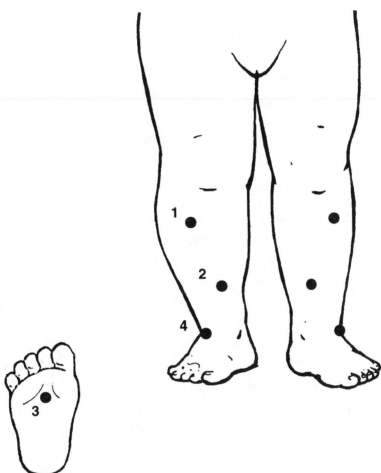

LEG POINT NAMES
Bubbling Spring (3)
Leg Three Miles (1)
Ravine Divide (4)
Three Yin Meeting (2)

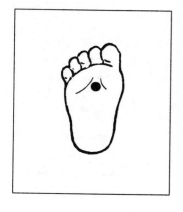

BUBBLING SPRING   YONG QUAN   (K 1)

Location: Sole of the foot at the centerline just below the ball (approximately one-third of the distance from the toes to the heel).

Technique: Press Rotate 50–100 times *or* Fingernail Press 5–10 times *or* Push with both thumbs from *Bubbling Spring* to the middle toe 50–100 times.

Action: Clear excess kidney heat, eliminate fretfulness, lead heat down. *Right foot:* Stop vomiting. *Left foot:* Stop diarrhea.

Indications: Headache, throat inflammation, convulsions, vomiting, diarrhea, fever, hot palms or soles, difficult urination, irritability.

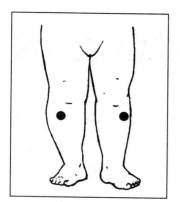

LEG THREE MILES   ZU SAN LI   (ST 36)

Location: Lower outside leg, three of the child's finger widths below the kneecap and one finger width to the side of the leg bone (tibia), between the two tendons.

Technique: Fingernail Press 5–10 times then Press Rotate 30–50 times *or* Press Rotate 100–300 times.

Action: Relieve chest, facilitate diaphragm movement, promote digestion, remove stagnation, eliminate spasm, relieve pain, tonify spleen, harmonize stomach, regulate abdominal qi.

Indications: Abdominal fullness or distension, stagnant cold stomach, intestinal gurgling, abdominal pain, convulsions, labored breathing, vomiting, diarrhea, weakness or atrophy of lower limbs.

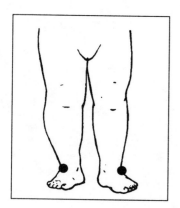

RAVINE DIVIDE   JIE XI   (ST 41)

Location: Top of the ankle, midway between the front midline of the leg and the outer ankle bone, the depression at the midpoint between two tendons approximately at the level of the ankle-bone tip.

Technique: Fingernail Press 5–10 times then Press Rotate 20–50 times *or* Press Rotate 100–200 times.

Action: Calm fright, relieve spasms, tonify spleen, harmonize stomach, stop diarrhea, remove stagnation.

Indications: Convulsions, vomiting, diarrhea, motor impairment of ankle joint.

THREE YIN MEETING SAN YIN JIAO (SP 6)

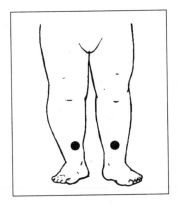

Location: Lower leg, inner side, three of the child's finger widths above the ankle-bone tip, behind the edge of the leg bone (tibia).

Technique: *Tonify:* Push up 20–30 times then Press Rotate 50–100 times *or* Press Rotate 100–200 times. *Clear:* Push down 20–30 times then Press Rotate 50–100 times *or* Fingernail Press 5–10 times then Press Rotate 20–30 times.

Action: Activate blood, calm liver, expel wind, clear meridians, regulate lower abdomen function, disperse pathogenic damp heat.

Indications: Bed-wetting (enuresis), urine retention, painful urination.

Note: To clear acute convulsions, Push down. To tonify chronic convulsions, Push up.

Head Region

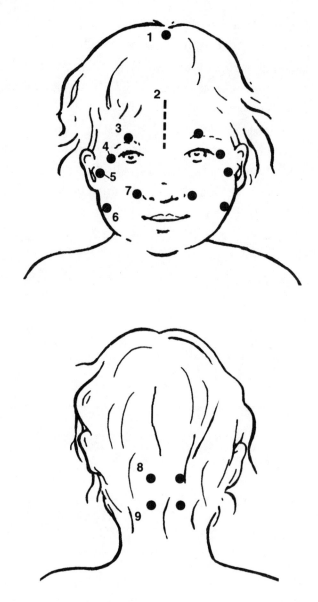

HEAD POINT NAMES

Brain Hollow (8)

Celestial Gate (2)

Ear Wind Gate (5)

Great Yang (4)

Jawbone (6)

Meeting of Hundreds (1)

Water Palace (3)

Welcome Fragrance (7)

Wind Pond (9)

Brain Hollow   Nao Kong   (GB 19)

Location: Back of the head directly above *Wind Pond,* two of the child's finger widths above the occipital ridge.

Technique: Fingernail Press 5–8 times then Press Rotate 10–20 times *or* Press Rotate 50–100 times.

Action: Expel wind, relieve pain.

Indications: Headache, epilepsy.

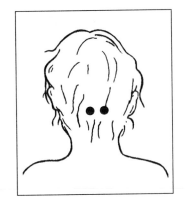

Celestial Gate   Tian Men

Location: Midline of the forehead from between the eyebrows to the hairline.

Technique: Push thumb over thumb briskly in one direction from the point between the eyebrows to the hairline 30–50 times *or* Press 3–7 times.

Action: Expel wind, relieve exterior, open orifices, sober and tranquilize mind, calm fright, soothe nerves, relieve headache.

Indications: Convulsions, fright, palpitation, common-cold fever without perspiration, vomiting, headache, dizziness, lassitude, depression, anxiety, terror, panic.

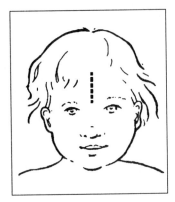

Ear Wind Gate   Er feng men

Location: Depression in front of the ear (easiest to find with child's mouth open).

Technique: Rotate Push both points simultaneously—forward to tonify, backward to clear.

Action: Tranquilize mind, calm fright.

Indications: Convulsions, tinnitus, deafness, toothache, earache.

GREAT YANG   TAI YANG   (X 1)

Location: Depression at the outside ends of the eyebrows.

Technique: Rotate Push 20–50 times. *Tonify:* Forward. *Clear:* Backward.

Action: Expel wind, clear heat, open orifices, calm fright.

Indications: Convulsions, fever, vexation, restlessness, common cold without perspiration, headache, eye pain, external pathogenically caused headache.

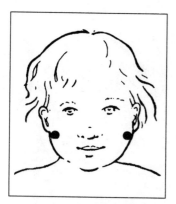

JAWBONE   JIA CHE   (ST 6)

Location: In the angle formed by the jaw joint.

Technique: Fingernail Press 5–10 times then Press Rotate 30–50 times *or* Press 5 times then Press Rotate 30 times.

Action: Open blockages and obstructions.

Indications: Eye and mouth deviations.

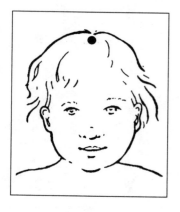

MEETING OF HUNDREDS   BAI HUI   (GV 20)

Location: Top of the head, at the peak of lines drawn from the tips of both ears.

Technique: Press Rotate 100–300 times *or* Fingernail Press 5 times then Press Rotate 30–50 times *or* Press 3–7 times then Press Rotate 30–50 times.

Action: Lift sunken yang and qi, ease mind, calm fright, open orifices, improve eyesight, soothe nerves, tonify qi.

Indications: Convulsions, epilepsy, headache, dizziness, diarrhea, bedwetting, blurred vision, nasal obstruction, prolapsed rectum, restlessness, crying, irritability, insomnia.

Note: Do not use with nausea or vomiting.

WATER PALACE   KAN GONG

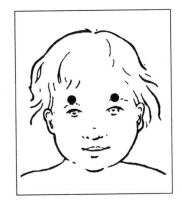

Location: Just above the eyebrow in a line with the pupil.

Technique: Push Apart 20–30 times *or* Fingernail Press 1 time, then Push Apart 20–30 times.

Action: Expel wind, disperse cold, open orifices, improve eyesight, induce perspiration, disperse pathogens from exterior, relieve headache.

Indications: External fever, convulsions, headache, eye redness and pain.

WELCOME FRAGRANCE   YING XIANG   (LI 20)

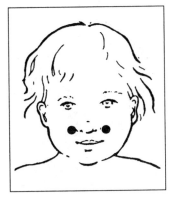

Location: Just to the side of each nostril, at the corner.

Technique: Fingernail Press 5–10 times then Press Rotate 20–40 times.

Action: Open orifices, activate meridians.

Indications: Eye or mouth deviations, stuffy nose, nasal discharge.

WIND POND   FENG QI   (GB 20)

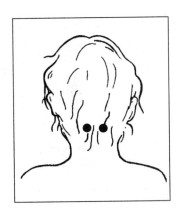

Location: Back of the head, below the base of the skull, in the depression between two muscles (sternocleidomastoid and trapezius).

Technique: Grasp 10–20 times *or* Fingernail Press simultaneously 10–20 times *or* Press Rotate 30–50 times.

Action: Induce perspiration, relieve exterior, expel wind, improve eyesight, disperse heat, expel wind or cold.

Indications: Neck pain or stiffness, headache, dizziness, fever without perspiration.

5
MASSAGE PLANS

THIS CHAPTER PRESENTS A COLLECTION OF MASSAGE PLANS for twenty-two common and relatively simple children's conditions. It is not a comprehensive list of all possible conditions, nor are all possible variations of each condition listed. My main purpose in this chapter is to present to you basic plans with which to begin. More complex or difficult conditions may also respond to massage, but should be evaluated by a professional first. Additional massage plans for these conditions may be found in my book *Chinese Pediatric Massage: A Practitioner's Guide*.

For each condition listed here I present a base plan along with variations for energetic discriminations of the condition. For example, under the Abdominal Pain massage plan, the base plan lists eleven points with variations added for differences from cold, deficiency, food retention, and summer heat.

One of the major benefits of the Chinese medical approach is the ability to shape the treatment to fit the characteristics of the individual. Here, each base massage plan includes the common points that all of the energetic conditions share. The variations section gives you suggestions on how you can tailor the base plan through additions or deletions to fit a specific situation. If you are uncertain about distinguishing between the different energetic types of the condition, using only the base plan will still be helpful for your child.

CHOOSING A MASSAGE PLAN

Find the condition that most closely describes your child's situation. Read through the different energetic descriptions, then observe your child, looking for relevant signs and symptoms according to these descriptions. Use the base plan and variations that most closely resemble your child's signs and symptoms.

The descriptions included with these massage plans may not exactly match every child's condition. The techniques and points are general enough to account for minor differences. However, if you have significant doubts or questions about your child's condition, consult with an appropriate health care professional.

ORDER OF POINTS

In general, points are grouped by region and performed in the following order: hands, arms, front of torso, back of torso, legs, and head. Points on both sides of the body are usually massaged.

If a point or technique is likely to cause discomfort because of its location or repetitive nature, it is best to leave this point for the end of the massage. A very useful beginning or end of the massage routine consists of using Push *Water Palace*, Push *Celestial Gate*, and Press Rotate *Great Yang*. Together these three points act to calm the child and consolidate the benefits of the other points you have used in the massage.

MASSAGE LENGTH

The length of a massage will be determined by the number of points selected and the number of technique repetitions necessary. In general, a full massage will last between 15 and 25 minutes. Remember that the techniques are performed in a very quick, brisk manner.

MASSAGE FREQUENCY

The frequency of massage depends on the severity and type of condition. The following are general guidelines:

Acute conditions: Daily
Severe conditions: Twice daily
Chronic or deficient conditions: Every other day

The number of massages necessary for a given condition will vary. In general, an acute condition will resolve in one to three massages. A chronic condition may take ten to twenty massages per month over a period of six to eight months. A more stubborn condition could require more massage. Additional factors, such as other medical treatments, diet, and herbal therapy, will have a significant impact on the length of the condition. There is no magic formula that will guarantee results; with good intentions and persistent effort, however, you should find these massage plans to be a useful guide for the care of common conditions.

MASSAGE MEDIUMS

Always use massage mediums to protect the delicate nature of the child's skin from the repetitive nature of the techniques. The medium may also have a therapeutic effect by its energetic nature. For example, the warming medium sesame oil would be used with a cold or deficient condition. A cooling medium such as cool water would be used with a hot or excessive condition. Appendix A lists a variety of mediums, their energetic natures, and indications for their use.

MASSAGE PLAN ARRANGEMENT

Massage plans are organized in the following format:

Title
Western medical description
Energetic description
Energetic patterns
Base massage plan
Variations
Massage medium

Titles are the common names for given conditions. Western medical descriptions are self-explanatory. The energetic description translates the Western information into corresponding energetic terminology. Where relevant, the energetic description is divided by energetic nature. Corresponding signs and symptoms are presented. Major signs used to differentiate among categories are in **bold.** These are general descriptions, signs, and symptoms, and may not include every possibility.

Point location illustrations are provided for each of the base massage plan points. The number in parentheses (1–14) following each point refers to the illustrations accompanying each plan; when necessary, the reader can return to pages 46–75 for full descriptions of point locations. Because the points given in the variations are not on the accompanying illustrations, the page number referring the reader back to that point's description appears in parentheses following the point name. Some of the illustrations are blank, indicating there are no points from the base plan in that region. This gives you the opportunity to mark point locations from the variations or from other sources as needed.

Sesame oil is the standard massage medium for most conditions. Cool or cold water is the easiest medium for hot or excessive conditions. Other massage mediums are listed with some of the variations. These are optional and are not required for each condition.

A complete massage consists of the base plan plus any relevant additions or deletions from variations. If it is not possible to perform a complete massage, select one to three points for a brief massage. An asterisk (*) is used to indicate the three main points of each base plan, which you can use for a brief massage.

ABDOMINAL PAIN

Description: Pain originating in the abdomen, possibly due to reduced function of abdominal organs.

Energetic: Attack of external cold, improper diet, congenital deficiency, deficient or cold spleen due to prolonged illness, summer damp or heat stagnation in spleen.

PATTERNS

Cold: Sudden onset, **pale complexion,** bluish lips, soft abdomen, **desires warmth,** loose stool, clear urine, cold sweat on forehead, cold limbs, vomiting, diarrhea.

Tongue: Pale, thin white coating.

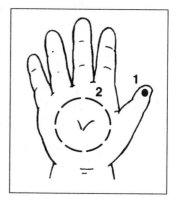

Cold/deficiency: Protracted and **continuous pain,** temporary relief after eating, desires warmth, aggravated with hunger, glossy and pale complexion, **emaciation,** weariness, feeble, cold limbs, loose stool, clear and copious urine.

Tongue: Pale with thick, white coating.

Food retention: **Foul breath odor,** belching, nausea, vomiting, **foul stool.**

Tongue: Red with thick, greasy coating.

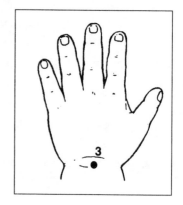

Summer heat: Recurrent abdominal pain, **hot abdomen,** dry stool, deep-colored urine, thirst, large intake of water.

Tongue: Red with yellow coating.

BASE PLAN

* Press Rotate *Spleen Meridian* (1)

Rotate Push *Inner Eight Symbols* (counterflow) (2)

Press Rotate *One Nestful Wind* (3)

* Push *Three Passes* (4)

Push *Below Ribs* (5)

* Rotate Push *Abdomen* (6)

Press Rotate *Bubbling Spring* (7)

Press Rotate *Ravine Divide* (8)

Press Rotate *Leg Three Miles* (9)

Push *Water Palace* (10)

Press Rotate (lightly) *Great Yang* (11)

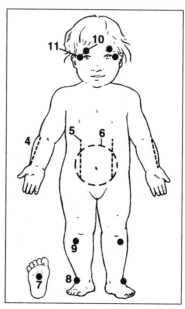

*Refers to main points for brief massage   ◆   Numbers on illustrations refer to base plan

Variations

With cold ADD:

Increase repetitions Push *Three Passes* (p. 58)

Press Rotate *External Palace of Labor* (p. 47)

Press Rotate *Spinal Column* (p. 67)

Medium: Ginger or scallion tea

With deficiency and cold ADD:

Push then Press Rotate *Four Transverse Lines* (p. 48)

Press Rotate *Two Horses* (p. 55)

Press Rotate to sides of *Spinal Column* (p. 67), especially *Spleen Back Point* (p. 68), *Stomach Back Point* (p. 68), and *Kidney Back Point* (p. 66)

Medium: Ginger or scallion tea

With food retention ADD:

Push (clear) *Stomach Meridian* (p. 55)

Press *Wood Gate* (p. 56)

Push (clear) *Large Intestine Meridian* (p. 51)

Medium: Chinese hawthorn tea

With summer heat ADD:

Push (clear) *Liver Meridian* (p. 51)

Push *Water of Galaxy* (p. 59)

Medium: Cold water

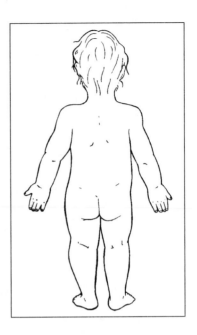

ASTHMA

Description: Labored breathing accompanied by wheezing caused by a spasming of the bronchial tubes or swelling of the mucous membranes.

Energetic: Congenital deficiency, weak constitution, attack of external pathogens. Chronic asthma weakens lungs, spleen, and kidneys with accumulated damp and phlegm in respiratory tract and body.

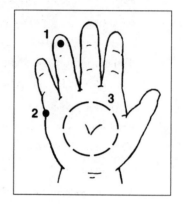

PATTERNS

Heat: **Red complexion,** thirst, **sticky yellow phlegm,** perspiration, deep-colored urine, constipation.

Tongue: Thin yellow or greasy yellow coating.

Cold: Emaciation, cold limbs, glossy and **pale complexion, lung phlegm dilute and white or clear,** dilute nasal discharge, clear urine, loose stool.

Tongue: Thin white or greasy white coating.

Kidney deficiency: Dizziness, **night sweats,** lower back ache, increased clear urine, aversion to cold, poor appetite, loose stool.

Tongue: Pale.

Lung deficiency: Cough, **weak voice, daytime perspiration,** infrequent speaking, aversion to cold, white complexion.

Tongue: Pale, normal.

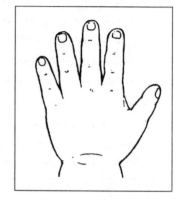

BASE PLAN

* Push (clear) *Lung Meridian* (1)

* Press Rotate *Palmar Small Transverse Line* (2)

Rotate Push *Inner Eight Symbols* (counterflow) (3)

Push Apart *Chest Center* (4)

Push *Celestial Chimney* (down) (5)

Press Rotate *Celestial Chimney* (6)

* Press Rotate *Calm Breath* (7)

Press Rotate *Spleen Back Point* (8)

Press Rotate *Lung Back Point* (9)

Push Apart *Scapula* (10)

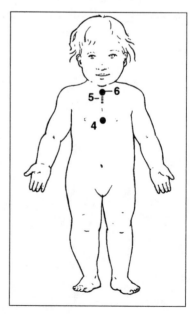

*Refers to main points for brief massage   ◆   Numbers on illustrations refer to base plan

VARIATIONS

WITH PHLEGM ADD:

Press Rotate *White Tendon* (p. 56)

Press Rotate *Five Digital Joints* (p. 47)

WITH HEAT ADD:

Push and then Press Rotate *Five Digital Joints* (p. 47)

Push *Water of Galaxy* (p. 59)

WITH COLD ADD:

Press Rotate *Kidney Meridian* (p. 50)

Press Rotate *External Palace of Labor* (p. 47)

Push *Three Passes* (p. 58)

WITH KIDNEY DEFICIENCY ADD:

Press Rotate *Two Horses* (p. 55)

Press Rotate *Kidney Meridian* (p. 50)

Push *Three Passes* (p. 58)

Press Rotate *Kidney Back Point* (p. 66)

Rotate Push *Abdomen* (p. 61)

Medium: Ginger tea

WITH LUNG DEFICIENCY DELETE:

Push (clear) *Lung Meridian* (p. 52)

ADD: Press Rotate *Lung Meridian* (p. 52)

Press Rotate *Kidney Meridian* (p. 50)

Push *Three Passes* (p. 58)

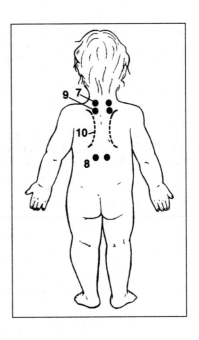

BED-WETTING (ENURESIS)

Description: Involuntary discharge of urine after the age when bladder control is expected (approximately three to five years old).

Energetic: Kidney or bladder qi deficiency, spleen or lung qi deficiency, damp or heat accumulation in liver meridian.

PATTERNS

Weak constitution: General deficient pattern, low energy, easily contracts colds, weak digestion, **low weight, slow growth,** pale complexion.

Tongue: Pale.

Spleen/lung deficient qi: **Emaciation,** pale complexion, listlessness, shortness of breath, **poor appetite,** dripping urine, frequent bed-wetting with small amounts of urine, loose stool.

Tongue: Pale, red with thin white coating.

Liver damp/heat: Irritability, night sweats, urgent and frequent urination by day, bed-wetting at night, **yellow and foul urine, red complexion and lips.**

Tongue: Thin yellow coating.

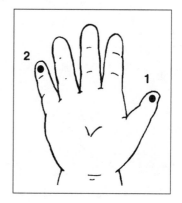

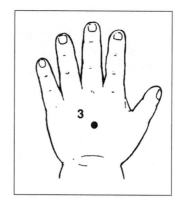

BASE PLAN

Press Rotate *Spleen Meridian* (1)

* Press Rotate *Kidney Meridian* (2)

Press Rotate *External Palace of Labor* (3)

Push *Three Passes* (4)

* Press Rotate *Elixir Field;* alternate with Rotate Push *Elixir Field* (5)

Press Rotate *Kidney Back Point* (6)

* Push *Bone of Seven Segments* (up) (7)

Press Rotate *Three Yin Meeting* (8)

Press Rotate *Meeting of Hundreds* (9)

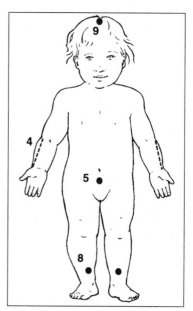

*Refers to main points for brief massage   ◆   Numbers on illustrations refer to base plan

VARIATIONS

WITH WEAK CONSTITUTION ADD:

Press Rotate on each side of *Spinal Column* (down)
   (p. 67)

Press Rotate *Two Horses* (p. 55)

Press Rotate *Life Gate* (p. 66)

Rub Palms Together then cover *Life Gate* (p. 66)

Medium: Ilex oil or dilute ginger tea

SPLEEN/LUNG DEFICIENT QI ADD:

Press Rotate *Lung Meridian* (p. 52)

Press Rotate *Spleen Back Point* (p. 68)

Press Rotate *Stomach Back Point* (p. 68)

Press Rotate *Lung Back Point* (p. 66)

WITH LIVER DAMP/HEAT DELETE:

Press Rotate *Kidney Meridian*

Press Rotate *Kidney Back Point*

Press Rotate *Meeting of Hundreds*

AND ADD:

Push (clear) *Liver Meridian* (p. 51)

Push (clear) *Large Intestine Meridian* (p. 51)

Push (clear) *Water of Galaxy* (p. 59)

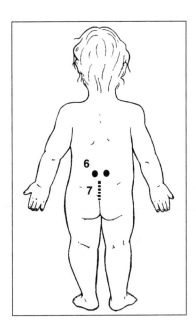

CHICKEN POX

Description: Acute viral disease with headache, fever, and malaise followed by red dotlike eruptions.

Energetic: Attack of seasonal pathogens and accumulated damp or heat.

PATTERNS

Mild case: Fever, headache, cough, poor appetite, stuffy nose, nasal discharge, **oval red eruptions with clear pus** in sparse distribution, slight itching.

Tongue: Red with thin white or yellow coating.

Severe case: Strong fever, red complexion and lips, mouth ulcers, listlessness, **dim purple eruptions with turbid pus** that are large, dense, and very itchy, deep-colored urine, dry stool.

Tongue: Red with yellow coating.

BASE PLAN

I. MILD CASE:

* Push (clear) *Lung Meridian* (1)

* Press Rotate *Kidney Meridian* (2)

Press Rotate *Small Celestial Center* (3)

* Press Rotate *One Nestful Wind* (4)

Rotate Push *Inner Eight Symbols* (5)

Push *Wood Gate* (6)

Push *Water of Galaxy* (7)

Press Rotate *Bubbling Spring* (8)

Medium: Scallion tea

II. SEVERE CASE:

* Press Rotate *Spleen Meridian* (9)

* Push Apart *Large Transverse Line* (10)

Press Rotate *Inner Palace of Labor* (11)

Press Rotate *Two Horses* (12)

Push *Six Hollow Bowels* (13)

* Push *Three Passes* (14)

Medium: Warm water or egg white

Note: When no new eruptions occur, delete Press Rotate *Spleen Meridian* and Push *Three Passes*.

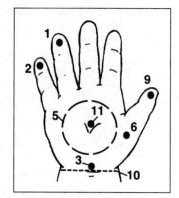

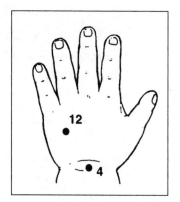

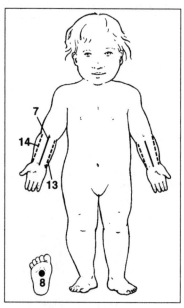

*Refers to main points for brief massage   ◆   Numbers on illustrations refer to base plan

VARIATIONS[†]

WITH HIGH FEVER DELETE:

Press Rotate *Spleen Meridian* (p. 54) and Push *Three Passes* (p. 59) until temperature reaches 100°F (38°C).

ADD: Push (clear) *Stomach Meridian* (p. 55)

WITH COUGH ADD:

Push (clear) *Liver Meridian* (p. 51)

Push Apart *Chest Center* (p. 62)

Press *Celestial Chimney* (p. 62)

WITH LOW FEVER ADD:

Push (clear) *Stomach Meridian* (p. 55)

Push (clear) *Lung Meridian* (p. 52)

Push *Water of Galaxy* (p. 59)

WITH ABDOMINAL PAIN ADD:

Push *Below Ribs* (p. 61)

Rotate Push *Abdomen* (p. 61)

WITH VOMITING ADD:

Push *Large Transverse Line* to *Wood Gate* (p. 56)

Press Rotate *Union Valley* (p. 56)

Press Rotate *Leg Three Miles* (p. 70)

[†] Any of the variations can be used with both mild and severe cases.

COLIC

Description: *Infantile colic* is a very general term used to describe a wide variety of symptoms occurring in children from birth to several years old. While the symptoms may vary widely, in general they all relate to some degree of pain, discomfort, restlessness, or crying, usually with no apparent cause.

Energetic: Two major aspects of colic may be involved in an individual child. The digestive system is considered inherently weak in infants and frequently may cause colic symptoms. Also, restlessness, anxiety, fearful sleep, or waking is explained as the child's energy not being settled or grounded properly in the body. An unusual, frightening experience may also be a source for colic symptoms. Usually, colic in the United States is related to digestive weakness (spleen deficiency). See appendix B for an external herbal colic remedy.

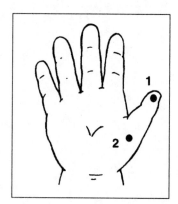

PATTERNS

Spleen deficiency: **Feeding-, digestion-, or elimination-related symptoms,** loose stool, pale lips, constant low feeble cry, poor or inconsistent appetite.

Tongue: Pale.

Heart fire: **Restlessness,** aversion to light or heat, sharp and loud crying, red complexion and lips, **hot body,** constipation.

Tongue: Red or red tipped.

Fright: **Sudden crying, easily alarmed,** sudden bluish or white complexion or lips.

Tongue: Normal or red.

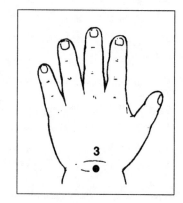

BASE PLAN

* Press Rotate *Spleen Meridian* (1)

Press Rotate *Wood Gate* (2)

Press Rotate *One Nestful Wind* (3)

* Push *Three Passes* (4)

* Rotate Push *Abdomen* (5)

Spinal Pinch Pull *Spinal Column* (6)

Press Rotate *Bubbling Spring* (7)

Press Rotate *Ravine Divide* (8)

Press Rotate *Leg Three Miles* (9)

Push *Water Palace* (10)

Push *Celestial Gate* (11)

Press Rotate *Great Yang* (12)

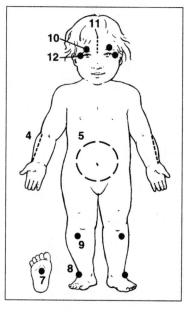

*Refers to main points for brief massage   ◆   Numbers on illustrations refer to base plan

VARIATIONS

WITH SPLEEN DEFICIENCY ADD:

Rotate Push *Inner Eight Symbols* (p. 49)

Press Rotate *External Palace of Labor* (p. 47)

WITH HEART FIRE ADD:

Push *Water of Galaxy* (p. 59)

Push Apart *Large Transverse Line* (p. 51)

WITH FRIGHT ADD:

Press Rotate *Inner Palace of Labor* (p. 50)

Press Rotate *Small Celestial Center* (p. 53)

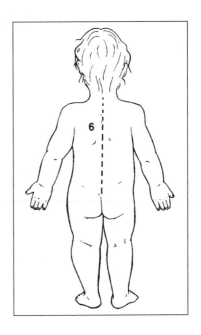

Description: General term for inflammation of the respiratory mucous membranes. May include congestion, watery discharge, sneezing, tearing.

Energetic: Attack of external pathogens, weak defensive qi, weather or seasonal changes.

PATTERNS

Wind/cold: **Light or no fever,** headache, no perspiration, **dilute nasal discharge,** unproductive cough.

Tongue: Pale, red with thin white coating.

Wind/heat: **Fever, turbid nasal discharge,** productive cough with yellow phlegm, throat pain, swelling, poor appetite, yellowish red urine, constipation.

Tongue: Red with yellow coating.

BASE PLAN

Push (clear) *Lung Meridian* (1)

* Push *Celestial Gate* (2)

* Rotate Push *Great Yang* (lightly) (3)

* Push *Water Palace* (4)

Grasp *Wind Pond* (5)

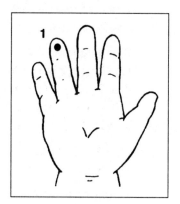

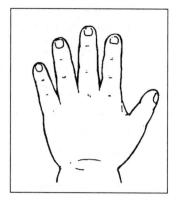

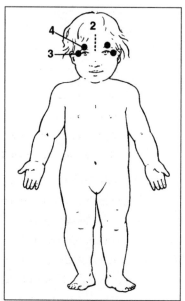

*Refers to main points for brief massage ◆ Numbers on illustrations refer to base plan

VARIATIONS

WITH WIND/COLD ADD:
Press Rotate *Two Leaf Doors* (p. 55)

Push *Three Passes* (p. 58)

WITH WIND/HEAT ADD:
Press Rotate *One Nestful Wind* (p. 53)

Press Rotate *Small Celestial Center* (p. 53)

Push *Water of Galaxy* (p. 59)

Medium: Peppermint tea

WITH RUNNY NOSE ADD:
Press Rotate *Welcome Fragrance* (p. 75)

TO INDUCE SWEAT ADD:
Grasp *Great Hammer* (p. 65)

Medium: Scallion or ginger tea

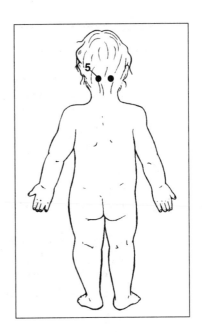

WITH FEVER ADD:
Rotate Push *Inner Palace of Labor* (p. 50)

Push then Press Rotate *Five Digital Joints* (p. 47)

Increase repetitions Push *Water Palace* (p. 75) and *Celestial Gate* (p. 73)

Push *Water of Galaxy* (p. 59)

Increase repetitions Push *Water Palace*, alternating fast and slow, light and medium pressure (p. 75)

Push *Spinal Column* (down) (p. 67)

WITH COUGH ADD:
Rotate Push *Inner Eight Symbols* (counterflow) (p. 49)

Push Apart *Chest Center* (p. 62)

Push *Celestial Chimney* (down) (p. 62)

WITH PHLEGM ADD:
Push *Wood Gate* (p. 56)

Push Apart *Large Transverse Line* (p. 51)

Press Rotate *Lung Back Point* (p. 66)

TO STRENGTHEN AFTER RECOVERY FROM COLD ADD:
Rotate Push *Inner Eight Symbols* (p. 49)

Push *Three Passes* (p. 58)

Rotate Push *Abdomen* (p. 61)

Press Rotate *Spleen Back Point* (p. 68)

Spinal Pinch Pull *Spinal Column* (up) (p. 67)

Press Rotate *Leg Three Miles* (p. 70)

Description: Sluggish, infrequent, or difficult bowel movements, with passage of hard or dry stool.

Energetic: Congenital excess or deficiency, lung or spleen patterns.

PATTERNS

Excess external heat: Dry stool, **thirst, red complexion,** abdominal distension, vomiting, fretfulness, painful and difficult bowel movements, relief after bowel movement, red complexion and lips.

Tongue: Red with thin yellow coating.

Deficient congenital qi: **Emaciated, thin build,** glossy and pale complexion, listless, feeble breath, low crying sound, painful and difficult bowel movements, pale and red lips.

Tongue: Pale, red

Spleen/lung deficiency: **Poor appetite,** weary, **sallow complexion,** emaciated.

Tongue: Pale with little coating.

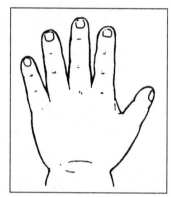

BASE PLAN

* Push (clear) *Large Intestine Meridian* (1)

Rotate Push *Inner Eight Symbols* (counterflow) (2)

* Press Rotate *Spleen Meridian* (3)

Push *Below Ribs* (4)

* Rotate Push *Abdomen* (5)

Push *Bone of Seven Segments* (down) (6)

Press Rotate *Tortoise Tail* (7)

Press Rotate *Leg Three Miles* (8)

Push *Water Palace* (9)

Press Rotate (lightly) *Great Yang* (10)

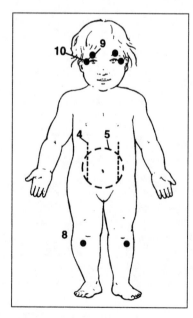

*Refers to main points for brief massage   ◆   Numbers on illustrations refer to base plan

VARIATIONS

WITH EXCESS EXTERNAL HEAT ADD:

Push *Water of Galaxy* (p. 59)

Press Rotate *Arm Yang Pool* (p. 58)

WITH DEFICIENT CONGENITAL QI ADD:

Press Rotate *Kidney Meridian* (p. 50)

Press Rotate *Two Horses* (p. 55)

WITH SPLEEN/LUNG DEFICIENCY ADD:

Press Rotate *Lung Meridian* (p. 52)

Press Rotate *Lung Back Point* (p. 66)

Press Rotate *Spleen Back Point* (p. 68)

Grasp *Shoulder Well* (p. 67)

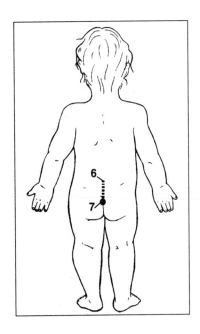

Description: Forceful, possibly violent exhalation effort preceded by an inspiration.

Energetic: Attack of external pathogens on lungs, deficient lung yin qi, deficient spleen causing phlegm.

PATTERNS

Wind/cold: Frequent coughing with **dilute white phlegm,** headache, fever, aversion to cold, **no perspiration,** itchy throat, body aches.

Tongue: Thin white coating.

Wind/heat: Chest oppression, **sticky yellow phlegm,** thirst, sore throat, turbid nasal discharge, fever, headache, **slight perspiration.**

Tongue: Thin yellow coating.

Lung heat: **Sudden recurrent cough, sticky phlegm,** dry throat, fever, thirst, red complexion and lips, deep-colored urine, dry stool, restlessness.

Tongue: Red without coating, little saliva.

Phlegm/damp: **Profuse dilute white phlegm,** chest fullness, no appetite, worse at night, listlessness.

Tongue: Pale with yellowish or white coating.

Yin deficiency: **Unproductive cough or difficult-to-expectorate phlegm,** itchy throat, hoarse voice, hot soles and palms, afternoon fever.

Tongue: Red with little coating.

Spleen/lung qi deficiency: **Feeble cough with dilute white phlegm,** glossy complexion, desires warmth, aversion to cold, shortness of breath, low voice.

Tongue: Pale, tender.

BASE PLAN

* Push (clear) *Lung Meridian* (1)

* Push then Press Rotate *Five Digital Joints* (2)

Rotate Push *Inner Eight Symbols* (counterflow) (3)

* Push *Celestial Chimney* (down) (4)

Push Apart *Scapula* (5)

Press Rotate *Lung Back Point* (6)

Push *Water Palace* (7)

Push *Great Yang* (8)

Push *Celestial Gate* (9)

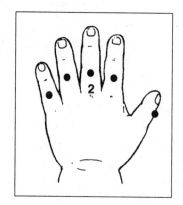

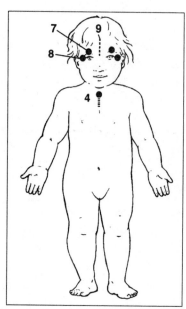

*Refers to main points for brief massage   ◆   Numbers on illustrations refer to base plan

VARIATIONS

WITH WIND/COLD ADD:

Push *Three Passes* (p. 58)

Grasp *Wind Pond* (p. 75)

Medium: Ginger juice

WITH WIND/HEAT ADD:

Press Rotate *One Nestful Wind* (p. 53)

Press Rotate *Small Celestial Center* (p. 53)

Push *Water of Galaxy* (p. 59)

Medium: Peppermint tea

WITH LUNG HEAT ADD:

Press Rotate *Palmar Small Transverse Line* (p. 53)

Press Rotate *Two Leaf Doors* (p. 55)

WITH PHLEGM/DAMP ADD:

Press Rotate *Spleen Meridian* (p. 54)

Press Rotate *White Tendon* (p. 56)

Push then Press Rotate *Four Transverse Lines* (p. 48)

WITH YIN DEFICIENCY ADD:

Press Rotate *Kidney Meridian* (p. 50)

Press Rotate *Two Horses* (p. 55)

Press Rotate *Bubbling Spring* (p. 70)

WITH SPLEEN/LUNG QI DEFICIENCY DELETE:

Push (clear) *Lung Meridian*

AND ADD:

Press Rotate *Spleen Meridian* (p. 54)

Press Rotate *Lung Meridian* (p. 52)

Press Rotate *Two Horses* (p. 55)

Push *Three Passes* (p. 58)

Press Rotate *Meeting of Hundreds* (p. 74)

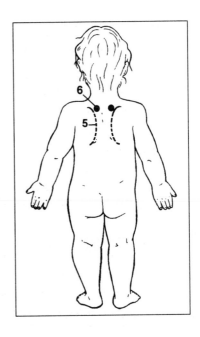

Description: Frequent bowel movements of loose or watery stool.

Energetic: Attack of external pathogens, immature or deficient spleen.

Diarrhea is a common condition in children due to their inherent condition of spleen weakness. Occasional short periods of diarrhea may be considered normal. A mild case of diarrhea may be defined as having few symptoms or other effects on the child and lasting a few days. A severe case of diarrhea is indicated by severe symptoms over a longer time period, dehydration, and a larger impact on the other energetic functions of the child.

PATTERNS

Cold/damp: Pale complexion and lips, **no thirst,** no dryness of mouth, **cold aversion,** cold limbs.

Tongue: Moist white coating.

Heat: Sudden onset, **thirst, hot body feeling,** perspiration.

Tongue: Greasy yellow coating.

Improper eating: Distension and pain of abdominal region, **relief after bowel movement.**

Tongue: Greasy.

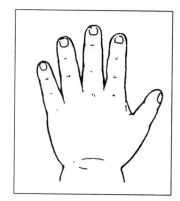

Fragile spleen: **Recurrent diarrhea, undigested food in stool,** abdominal fullness, no thirst, emaciation, listlessness.

Tongue: Pale with thin coating.

Chronic: A simple case of diarrhea due to external factors or temporary spleen or kidney deficiency that does not resolve quickly. Symptoms will vary according to energetic causes.

BASE PLAN

Press Rotate *Spleen Meridian* (1)

* Push (clear) *Small Intestine Meridian* (2)

Rotate Push *Inner Eight Symbols* (3)

Push *Three Passes* (4)

Push *Below Ribs* (5)

* Rotate Push *Abdomen* (6)

* Push *Bone of Seven Segments* (up) (7)

Press Rotate *Bubbling Spring* (8)

Press Rotate *Ravine Divide* (9)

Press Rotate *Leg Three Miles* (10)

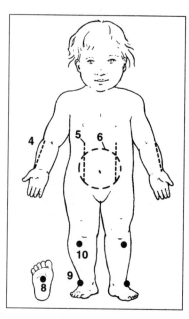

*Refers to main points for brief massage   ◆   Numbers on illustrations refer to base plan

VARIATIONS

WITH COLD AND/OR DAMP ADD:

Increase repetitions Push *Three Passes* (p. 58)

Rub Palms Together, cover *Elixir Field* (p. 63)

WITH HEAT DELETE:

Push *Three Passes*

ADD: Push (clear) *Stomach Meridian*

Push (clear) *Large Intestine Meridian*

Push *Six Hollow Bowels* (p. 58)

WITH IMPROPER EATING ADD:

Push (clear) *Large Intestine Meridian* (p. 51)

Increase repetitions Push *Below Ribs* (p. 61)

Grasp *Abdominal Corner* (p. 61)

Medium: Chinese hawthorn tea

WITH FRAGILE SPLEEN ADD:

Increase repetitions Press Rotate *Spleen Meridian* (p. 54)

Press Rotate *Kidney Meridian* (p. 50)

Press Rotate *Wood Gate* (p. 56)

Press Rotate *Meeting of Hundreds* (p. 74)

Press Rotate *Spinal Column* (p. 67), with emphasis on *Spleen Back Point* (p. 68) and *Stomach Back Point* (p. 68)

WITH CHRONIC DIARRHEA ADD:

Press Rotate *Meeting of Hundreds* (p. 74)

Press Rotate *Tortoise Tail* (p. 68)

Medium: Ginger tea

WITH VOMITING ADD:

Press Rotate *Union Valley* (p. 56)

Fingernail Press *Maternal Cheek* (p. 52)

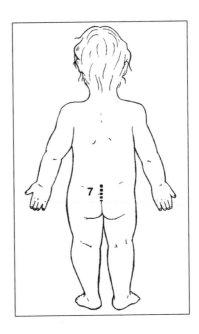

DIGESTIVE DIFFICULTIES

Description: Indigestion, loss of appetite, incomplete or imperfect digestion process, lack of desire to eat.

Energetic: Improper eating habits, congenital or postnatal spleen deficiency.

PATTERNS

Spleen damp: Poor appetite, nausea, vomiting, **abdominal distension,** listlessness, no thirst, loose stool.

Tongue: Red with thin, greasy yellow coating.

Stomach/spleen deficiency: Sallow complexion, **emaciation,** feebleness, frequent diarrhea.

Tongue: Pale with little coating.

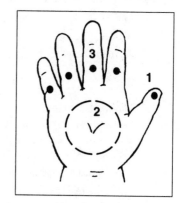

BASE PLAN

* Press Rotate *Spleen Meridian* (1)

Rotate Push *Inner Eight Symbols* (2)

Fingernail Press then Press Rotate *Four Transverse Lines* (3)

* Push *Three Passes* (4)

Push *Below Ribs* (5)

* Rotate Push *Abdomen* (6)

Spinal Pinch Pull *Spinal Column* (up) (7)

Press Rotate on each side of *Spinal Column,* especially *Spleen Back Point* and *Stomach Back Point* (8)

Press Rotate *Bubbling Spring* (9)

Press Rotate *Ravine Divide* (10)

Press Rotate *Leg Three Miles* (11)

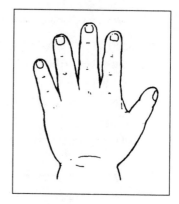

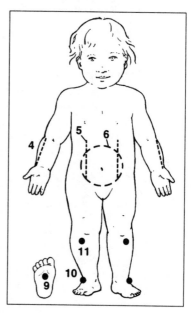

*Refers to main points for brief massage   ◆   Numbers on illustrations refer to base plan

VARIATIONS

WITH SPLEEN DAMP ADD:

Push Apart *Large Transverse Line* (p. 51)

Push *Wood Gate* (p. 56)

Push *Water of Galaxy* (p. 59)

Medium: Scallion or ginger tea

WITH STOMACH/SPLEEN DEFICIENCY ADD:

Press Rotate *One Nestful Wind* (p. 53)

Press Rotate *Small Celestial Center* (p. 53)

Press Rotate *External Palace of Labor* (p. 47)

CHRONIC ADD:

Press Rotate *Two Horses* (p. 55)

WITH CONSTIPATION ADD:

Press Rotate (clear) *Large Intestine Meridian* (p. 51)

Push *Bone of Seven Segments* (down) (p. 65)

WITH VOMITING ADD:

Fingernail Press *Maternal Cheek* (p. 52)

Press Rotate *Union Valley* (p. 56)

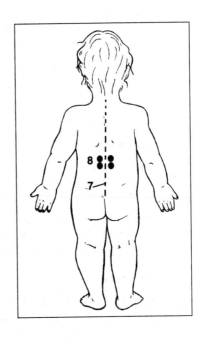

Description: Pain originating in ear.

Energetic: Attack of external pathogenic wind, cold, or heat; weak defensive qi; gallbladder or liver inflammation or weakness.

PATTERNS

Cold: **Aversion to cold,** headache, no perspiration, dilute nasal discharge.

Tongue: Pale, red.

BASE PLAN

* Push (clear) *Gallbladder Meridian* (1)

Press Rotate *Two Leaf Doors* (2)

* Push *Six Hollow Bowels* (3)

Press Rotate *Ear Wind Gate* (4)

* Grasp *Wind Pond* (5)

Push *Water Palace* (6)

Push *Celestial Gate* (7)

Press Rotate (lightly) *Great Yang* (8)

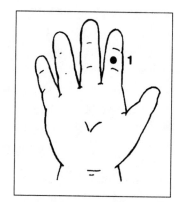

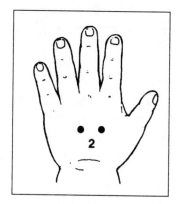

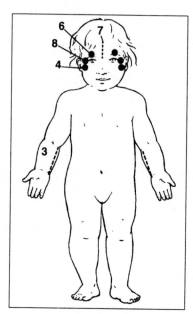

*Refers to main points for brief massage ◆ Numbers on illustrations refer to base plan

VARIATIONS

WITH FEVER ADD:

Press Rotate *Inner Palace of Labor* (p. 50)

Push *Water of Galaxy* (p. 59)

WITH COLD ADD:

Press Rotate *Small Celestial Center* (p. 53)

Rotate Push *Inner Eight Symbols* (p. 49)

Press Rotate *Welcome Fragrance* (p. 75)

WITH POOR DIGESTION AND/OR DIARRHEA ADD:

Press Rotate *Spleen Meridian* (p. 54)

Push *Below Ribs* (p. 61)

Rotate Push *Abdomen* (p. 61)

Press Rotate *Bubbling Spring* (p. 70)

Press Rotate *Ravine Divide* (p. 70)

Press Rotate *Leg Three Miles* (p. 70)

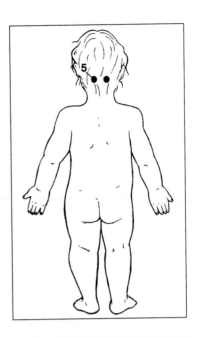

Description: Elevation of body temperature above normal.

Energetic: Fever results in the struggle between defensive qi and external pathogenic factors.

PATTERNS

There are many causes of fever; listed here are those involving external pathogens only.

Wind/cold: **Cold aversion,** no perspiration, **clear nasal discharge,** headache, itchy throat.

Tongue: Thin white coating.

Wind/heat: **High fever,** perspiration, headache, **thick nasal discharge,** swollen red throat, dry mouth, thirst.

Tongue: Red with thin white or yellow coating.

Lung heat: **Cough,** fever, aversion to cold, **sore throat,** stuffy or runny nose with yellow mucus, headache, body aches, slight sweating, thirst, swollen tonsils.

Tongue: Red with thin white or yellow coating.

Stomach/spleen deficiency: Sallow complexion, sleepiness, feebleness, **poor appetite,** abdominal distension, **loose stool,** restlessness at night, pale lips.

Tongue: Thick greasy white coating.

Summer heat: **Aversion to heat,** sweating, headache, **scanty dark urine,** dry lips, thirst.

Tongue: Red.

Kidney deficiency: **Listlessness,** reddened eyes, **feverish at soles of feet,** aversion to clothes, dizziness, limb weakness.

Tongue: Red with thin coating.

BASE PLAN

Fingernail Press *Old Dragon* (1)

Rotate Push *Inner Palace of Labor* (2)

Push *Six Hollow Bowels* (3)

* Press Rotate *Wind Pond* (4)

* Push *Spinal Column* (down) (5)

Push *Celestial Gate* (6)

* Push *Water Palace* (7)

Press Rotate (lightly) *Great Yang* (8)

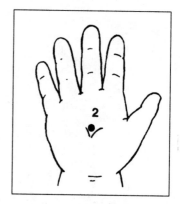

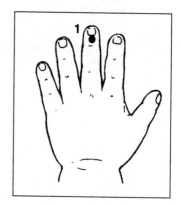

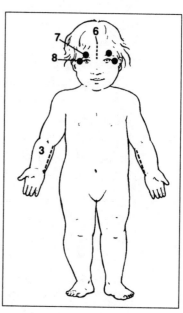

*Refers to main points for brief massage   ♦   Numbers on illustrations refer to base plan

VARIATIONS

WITH WIND/COLD ADD:

Press Rotate *Two Leaf Doors* (p. 55)

Press Rotate *One Nestful Wind* (p. 53)

Push *Three Passes* (p. 58)

Medium: Ginger juice

WITH WIND/HEAT ADD:

Push (clear) *Lung Meridian* (p. 52)

Push then Press Rotate *Five Digital Joints* (p. 47)

Push *Water of Galaxy* (p. 59)

Medium: Peppermint tea

WITH LUNG HEAT ADD:

Push (clear) *Lung Meridian* (p. 52)

Push (clear) *Large Intestine Meridian* (p. 51)

Push (clear) *Stomach Meridian* (p. 55)

Press Rotate *Small Celestial Center* (p. 53)

Press Rotate *One Nestful Wind* (p. 53)

Medium: Cool water

WITH STOMACH/SPLEEN DEFICIENCY ADD:

Press Rotate *Lung Meridian* (p. 52)

Push *Below Ribs* (p. 61)

Rotate Push *Abdomen* (p. 61)

Press Rotate *Spleen Back Point* (p. 68)

Press Rotate *Bubbling Spring* (p. 70)

Press Rotate *Ravine Divide* (p. 70)

Press Rotate *Leg Three Miles* (p. 70)

WITH SUMMER HEAT ADD:

Press Rotate *Kidney Meridian* (p. 50)

Press Rotate *Small Celestial Center* (p. 53)

Press Rotate *One Nestful Wind* (p. 53)

Press *Wood Gate* (p. 56)

Increase repetitions Push *Six Hollow Bowels* (p. 58)

Medium: Cool water

WITH KIDNEY DEFICIENCY ADD:

Press Rotate *Two Horses* (p. 55)

Press Rotate *Inner Palace of Labor* (p. 50)

Press Rotate *Spleen Meridian* (p. 54)

Push *Water of Galaxy* (p. 59)

Press Rotate *Bubbling Spring* (p. 70)

Press Rotate *Leg Three Miles* (p. 70)

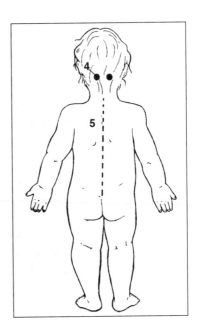

Description: Preventive care for a generally healthy child in order to maintain good health and strengthen the constitution.

PATTERNS

Choosing points in addition to the base massage plan will depend on an individual assessment of each child. Using the basic energetic assessment skills, look for organ systems with a tendency toward deficiency or excess. Add points related to those organs.

BASE PLAN

* Press Rotate *Spleen Meridian* (1)

  Rotate Push *Inner Eight Symbols* (2)

* Push *Three Passes* (3)

* Rotate Push *Abdomen* (4)

  Spinal Pinch Pull *Spinal Column* (up) (5)

  Press Rotate *Bubbling Spring* (6)

  Press Rotate *Ravine Divide* (7)

  Press Rotate *Leg Three Miles* (8)

  Push *Water Palace* (9)

  Press Rotate (lightly) *Great Yang* (10)

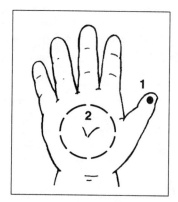

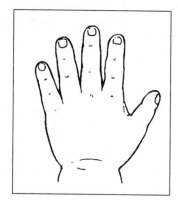

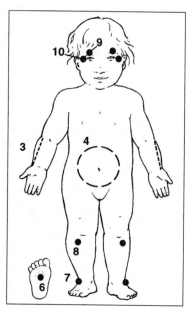

*Refers to main points for brief massage   ◆   Numbers on illustrations refer to base plan

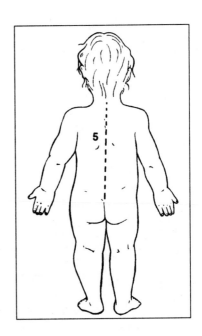

HEADACHE

Description: Different qualities of pain in various regions of the head, acute or chronic.

Energetic: There are many different patterns involving headache. Only external pathogenic causes are presented here.

PATTERNS

Wind/cold: Ache in neck and back, **aversion to wind and cold, dilute nasal discharge,** no thirst.

Tongue: Pale, red with thin white coating.

Wind/heat: Distended pain in head, **aversion to wind and heat,** flushed face, conjunctivitis, thirst, desire for drinks, **turbid nasal discharge,** dry stool, yellow urine.

Tongue: Red with yellow coating.

Phlegm/turbidity: Eye distension, drooping eyelids, desire to keep eyes closed, **nausea,** vomiting sputum and saliva, **chest oppression,** epigastric region fullness.

Tongue: Red with greasy yellow coating.

BASE PLAN

Press Rotate *Two Leaf Doors* (1)

* Press Rotate *Union Valley* (2)

Press Rotate *Brain Hollow* (3)

* Grasp *Wind Pond* (4)

Push *Celestial Gate* (5)

* Push *Water Palace* (6)

Press Rotate (lightly) *Great Yang* (7)

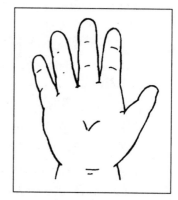

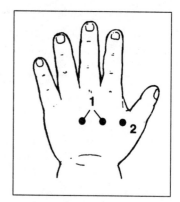

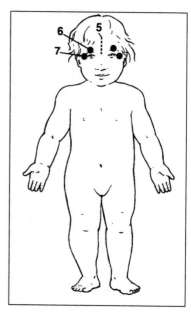

*Refers to main points for brief massage ◆ Numbers on illustrations refer to base plan

VARIATIONS

WITH WIND/COLD ADD:

Press Rotate *One Nestful Wind* (p. 53)

Press Rotate *Small Celestial Center* (p. 53)

Medium: Ginger or scallion tea

WITH WIND/HEAT ADD:

Push (clear) *Lung Meridian* (p. 52)

Press Rotate *Kidney Line* (p. 50)

Push *Water of Galaxy* (p. 59)

Medium: Peppermint tea

WITH PHLEGM/TURBIDITY ADD:

Press Rotate *External Palace of Labor* (p. 47)

Press Rotate *Spleen Meridian* (p. 54)

Push then Press Rotate *Small Transverse Lines* (p. 54)

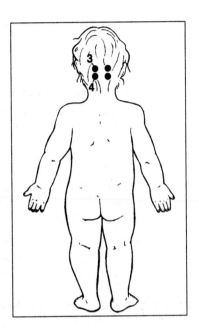

MEASLES

Description: Acute infectious disease with fever, malaise, sneezing, congestion, cough, conjunctivitis, red eruptions over entire body.

Energetic: Lung, spleen, and sometimes heart may be affected by resulting fever and depletion of fluids.

PATTERNS

Favorable course: Three to four days after onset, even distribution of eruptions (distinct red, circular spots). Spots appear, then subside.

BASE PLAN

* Push (clear) *Lung Meridian* (1)
* Press Rotate *Kidney Meridian* (2)
* Push *Three Passes* (3)
  Press Rotate *Lung Back Point* (4)
  Press Rotate *Spleen Back Point* (5)
  Press Rotate *Stomach Back Point* (6)
  Push *Water Palace* (7)
  Push *Celestial Gate* (8)
  Press Rotate (lightly) *Great Yang* (9)

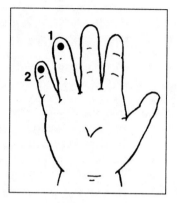

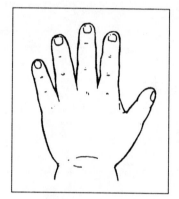

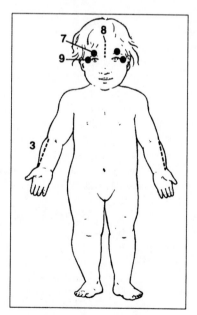

*Refers to main points for brief massage ◆ Numbers on illustrations refer to base plan

VARIATIONS

EARLY SYMPTOMS STAGE ADD:

Push back and forth *Liver Meridian* (p. 51)

Press Rotate *Small Celestial Center* (p. 53)

Press Rotate *One Nestful Wind* (p. 53)

Push *Water of Galaxy* (p. 59)

Medium: Dilute ginger juice

ERUPTION STAGE ADD:

Press Rotate *Two Leaf Doors* (p. 55)

Press Rotate *Small Celestial Center* (p. 53)

Press Rotate *One Nestful Wind* (p. 53)

Medium: Scute tea

RECOVERY STAGE ADD:

Press Rotate *Spleen Meridian* (p. 54)

Push *Below Ribs* (p. 61)

Rotate Push *Abdomen* (p. 61)

Press Rotate *Leg Three Miles* (p. 70)

Press Rotate (lightly) *Meeting of Hundreds* (p. 74)

SPECIFIC POINTS TO PROMOTE ERUPTIONS:

Press Rotate *Small Celestial Center* (p. 53)

Press Rotate *Spleen Meridian* (p. 54)

Press Rotate *Two Leaf Doors* (p. 55)

Push *Three Passes* (p. 58)

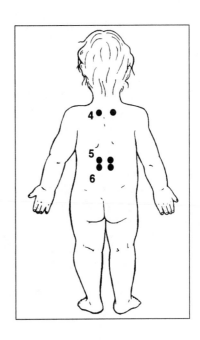

Description: Acute, contagious, febrile disease with inflammation of the neck glands.

Energetic: External attack of wind/heat, accumulated stagnant damp/heat of gallbladder meridian.

PATTERNS

Wind/heat: Fever, headache, pain in cheeks, pain with chewing, poor appetite.

Tongue: Red with **thin white or light yellow coating.**

Toxic heat: Fever, headache, dry mouth, **nausea,** vomiting, listlessness, cheek swelling, pain, constipation, deep-colored urine.

Tongue: Red with **very yellow coating.**

BASE PLAN

* Push (clear) *Liver Meridian* (1)

* Press Rotate *Small Celestial Center* (2)

* Press *Wood Gate* (3)

Push *Six Hollow Bowels* (4)

Push *Water of Galaxy* (5)

Grasp *Wind Pond* (6)

Press Rotate *Jawbone* (7)

Press Rotate *Bubbling Spring* (8)

Push *Water Palace* (9)

Press Rotate (lightly) *Great Yang* (10)

Push *Celestial Gate* (11)

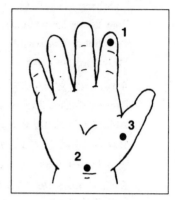

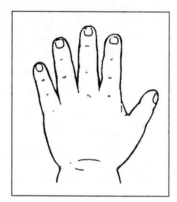

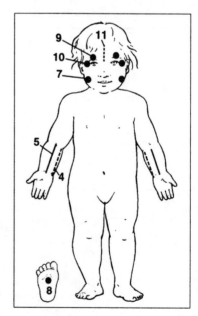

*Refers to main points for brief massage   ◆   Numbers on illustrations refer to base plan

VARIATIONS

WITH WIND/HEAT **ADD:**

Push (clear) *Lung Meridian* (p. 52)

Press Rotate *Inner Palace of Labor* (p. 50)

Press Rotate *Two Leaf Doors* (p. 55)

Medium: Scallion tea

WITH TOXIC/HEAT **ADD:**

Push Apart *Large Transverse Line* (p. 51)

Push then Press Rotate *Four Transverse Lines* (p. 48)

Press Rotate *Arm Yang Pool* (p. 58)

Medium: Egg white

WITH SWOLLEN TESTICLES **ADD** (IN CONJUNCTION WITH OTHER THERAPIES):

Press Rotate *Two Horses* (p. 55)

Press Rotate *Kidney Line* (p. 50)

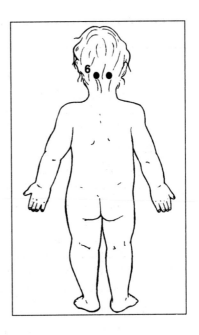

NIGHT CRYING

Description: Sudden crying out at night while sleeping.

Energetic: Congenital deficiency of spleen or stomach, postnatal malnutrition, excess heart fire, fright.

PATTERNS

Deficient stomach and/or spleen: Glossy and **pale complexion, pale lips,** timidity, cold limbs and abdomen, constant low and feeble cry, poor appetite, loose stool.

Tongue: Pale, thin white coating.

Heart fire: Restlessness, aversion to light, sharp loud crying, **red complexion and lips,** hot body, constipation, deep-colored urine.

Tongue: Red tip and sides, white coating.

Fright: Sudden crying, **easily alarmed,** sudden bluish or white complexion and lips.

Tongue: Normal.

BASE PLAN

Push Apart *Large Transverse Line* (1)

* Press Rotate *Small Celestial Center* (2)

* Press Rotate *Small Transverse Lines* (3)

Push *Celestial Gate* (4)

* Push *Water Palace* (5)

Press Rotate (lightly) *Great Yang* (6)

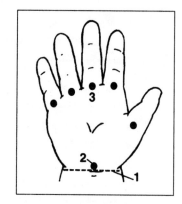

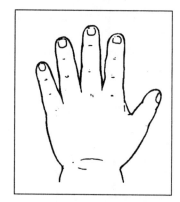

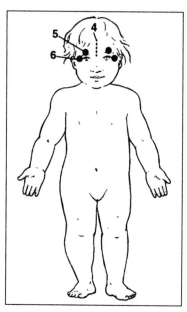

*Refers to main points for brief massage   ◆   Numbers on illustrations refer to base plan

VARIATIONS

WITH DEFICIENT STOMACH/SPLEEN ADD:

Press Rotate *Spleen Meridian* (p. 54)

Push *Three Passes* (p. 58)

Push *Below Ribs* (p. 61)

Rotate Push *Abdomen* (p. 61)

Medium: Ginger or scallion tea

WITH HEART FIRE ADD:

Push (clear) *Lung Meridian* (p. 52)

Push *Water of Galaxy* (p. 59)

Medium: Scute tea or peanut oil

WITH FRIGHT ADD:

Fingernail Press *Inner Palace of Labor* (p. 50)

Rotate Push *Inner Eight Symbols* (p. 49)

Medium: Peanut oil

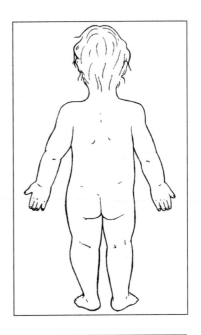

RUBELLA (GERMAN MEASLES)

Description: Acute infectious disease similar to scarlet fever and measles but differing in the short course, the slight fever, and lack of aftereffects.

Energetic: Weak exterior defenses allow for attack by seasonal pathogens of wind or heat.

BASE PLAN

I. DURING ERUPTIONS:

* Press Rotate *Spleen Meridian* (1)

Press Rotate *Small Celestial Center* (2)

* Press Rotate *One Nestful Wind* (3)

* Push (clear) *Lung Meridian* (4)

Push *Three Passes* (5)

Grasp *Wind Pond* (6)

Grasp *Shoulder Well* (7)

II. AFTER ERUPTIONS:

* Press Rotate *Kidney Meridian* (8)

Press Rotate *Spleen Meridian* (1)

Press Rotate *Kidney Line* (9)

* Push *Wood Gate* (10)

Push Apart *Large Transverse Line* (11)

Press Rotate *Small Celestial Center* (2)

* Push *Water of Galaxy* (12)

Medium: Scallion tea

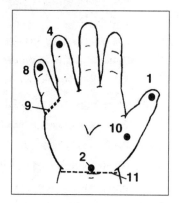

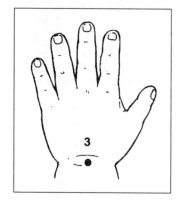

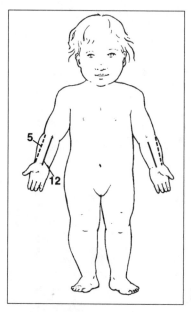

*Refers to main points for brief massage   ♦   Numbers on illustrations refer to base plan

VARIATIONS[†]

WITH HIGH FEVER DELETE:

Push *Water of Galaxy* (p. 59)

AND ADD:

Push (clear) *Lung Meridian* (p. 52)

Rotate Push *Inner Palace of Labor* (p. 50)

Push *Six Hollow Bowels* (p. 58)

WITH POOR APPETITE ADD:

Push (clear) *Stomach Meridian* (p. 55)

Push *Below Ribs* (p. 61)

Rotate Push *Abdomen* (p. 61)

WITH SORE THROAT ADD:

Press *Celestial Chimney* (p. 62)

Press Rotate *Union Valley* (p. 56)

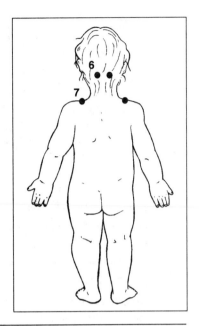

[†]Variations may be used either during or after eruptions.

Description: Inflammation of the throat, tonsils, pharynx, or larynx.

Energetic: External pathogenic attack of wind/cold or wind/heat.

BASE PLAN

* Push (clear) *Lung Meridian* (1)

Press Rotate *Union Valley* (2)

Rotate Push *Inner Eight Symbols* (counterflow) (3)

* Push *Water of Galaxy* (4)

* Grasp *Wind Pond* (5)

Press *Celestial Chimney* (6)

Push *Celestial Gate* (7)

Push *Water Palace* (8)

Press Rotate (lightly) *Great Yang* (9)

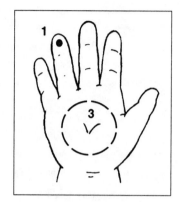

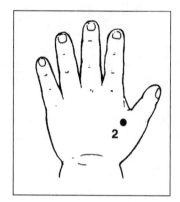

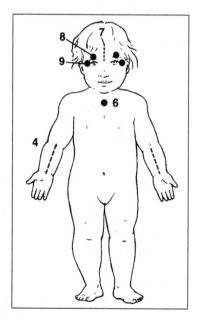

*Refers to main points for brief massage ◆ Numbers on illustrations refer to base plan

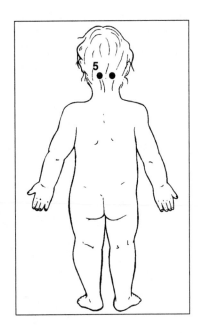

Description: Eruption of teeth through gums; pain in or around tooth.

Energetic: Attack of external pathogens, uprising stomach fire, deficient fire due to depletion of kidney yin.

PATTERNS

Excess: Bad odor on breath, **even swelling of gum and cheek,** headache, fever, constipation.

Tongue: Yellow coating.

Deficiency: Vague toothache, **no swelling of gum or cheek**

Tongue: Glossy with no coating.

BASE PLAN

* Press Rotate *Kidney Meridian* (1)

* Press Rotate *Small Celestial Center* (2)

  Press Rotate or Fingernail Press *Chief Tendon* (3)

* Push *Water Palace* (4)

  Press Rotate *Great Yang* (5)

  Push *Celestial Gate* (6)

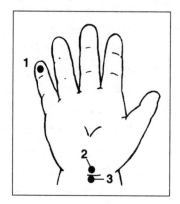

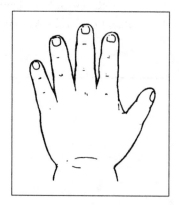

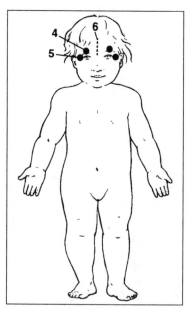

*Refers to main points for brief massage ♦ Numbers on illustrations refer to base plan

VARIATIONS

TOOTHACHE WITH DEFICIENCY ADD:

Press Rotate *Two Horses* (p. 55)

Press Rotate *Union Valley* (p. 56)

Press Rotate *Spleen Meridian* (p. 54)

TOOTHACHE WITH EXCESS ADD:

Press Rotate *One Nestful Wind* (p. 53)

Push *Water of Galaxy* (p. 59)

Press Rotate *Jawbone* (p. 74)

PAIN RELIEF POINTS ADD:

Press Rotate *Union Valley* (p. 56)

Push *Six Hollow Bowels* (p. 58)

Press Rotate *Leg Three Miles* (p. 70)

Press Rotate *Ear Wind Gate* (p. 73)

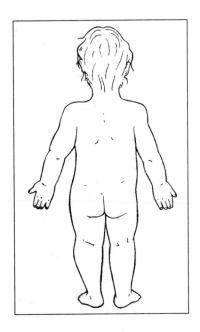

THRUST (APHTHA)

Description: Infection of mouth or throat, white patches and ulcers, sometimes accompanied by fever and gastrointestinal inflammation.

Energetic: Excess or deficient yin fire: affecting heart, spleen, or kidney.

PATTERNS

Excess fire: **Red complexion and lips,** restlessness, white ulcers in mouth and on tongue, constipation, deep-colored urine.

Tongue: Red tipped.

Deficiency fire: **Weakness,** timidity, **pale complexion with red eyes,** hot palms and soles, no thirst, low fever, night sweat.

Tongue: Red with little coating.

BASE PLAN

* Push (clear) *Small Intestine Meridian* (1)

Press Rotate *Chief Tendon* (2)

Push *Wood Gate* (3)

* Push then Press Rotate *Small Transverse Lines* (4)

Press Rotate *Small Celestial Center* (5)

* Push *Water of Galaxy* (6)

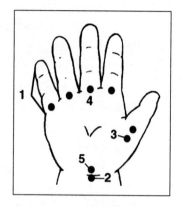

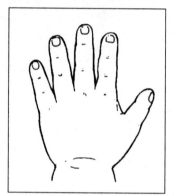

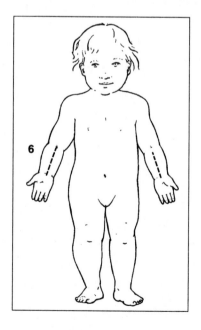

*Refers to main points for brief massage ◆ Numbers on illustrations refer to base plan

VARIATIONS

WITH EXCESS FIRE ADD:

Push (clear) *Stomach Meridian* (p. 55)

Push (clear) *Lung Meridian* (p. 52)

Push Apart *Large Transverse Line* (p. 51)

Press Rotate *Inner Palace of Labor* (p. 50)

WITH DEFICIENCY FIRE ADD:

Press Rotate *Kidney Meridian* (p. 50)

Press Rotate *Spleen Meridian* (p. 54)

Rotate Push *Inner Eight Symbols* (p. 49)

Press Rotate *Two Horses* (p. 55)

Push *Below Ribs* (p. 61)

Rotate Push *Abdomen* (p. 61)

Spinal Pinch Pull *Spinal Column* (p. 67), especially
Spleen Back Point (p. 68) and *Kidney Back
Point* (p. 66)

Medium: Scallion tea

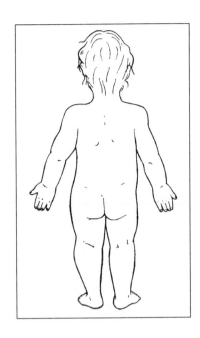

Description: Ejection through mouth of stomach contents.

Energetic: Attack of external pathogens, overeating or overdrinking, falling, fright, accumulation of heat or cold in stomach from congenital deficiency or deficient stomach qi.

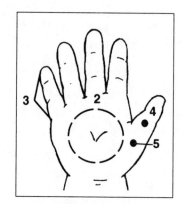

PATTERNS

Wind/cold: Sudden onset, frequent vomiting, **cold aversion, no perspiration.**

Tongue: Pale, red.

Wind/heat: Sudden onset, frequent vomiting, **fever or chills,** perspiration, headache, itchy throat.

Tongue: Red with thin greasy white or yellow coating.

Abnormal diet: Fullness, pain in stomach region, **foul gas belching,** sour putrid vomiting, fretfulness, insomnia, constipation or diarrhea, symptoms relieved with vomiting.

Tongue: Thick with greasy coating.

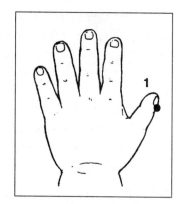

Stomach heat: Vomiting soon after eating, **desires liquids,** fretfulness, restlessness, **red complexion and lips,** constipation, deep-colored urine.

Tongue: Red with yellow coating.

Stomach cold: Recurrent vomiting, **clear dilute vomit without foul odor,** pale complexion and lips, cold limbs, continuous abdominal pain, loose stool.

Tongue: Pale with white coating.

BASE PLAN

* Fingernail Press *Maternal Cheek* (1)

Rotate Push (counterflow) *Inner Eight Symbols* (2)

Push (clear) *Small Intestine Meridian* (3)

Push (clear) *Stomach Meridian* (4)

* Press *Wood Gate* (5)

Push *Below Ribs* (6)

Rotate Push *Abdomen* (7)

Press Rotate *Spleen Back Point* (8)

Press Rotate *Bubbling Spring* (9)

Press Rotate *Ravine Divide* (10)

* Press Rotate *Leg Three Miles* (11)

Push *Water Palace* (12)

Press Rotate (lightly) *Great Yang* (13)

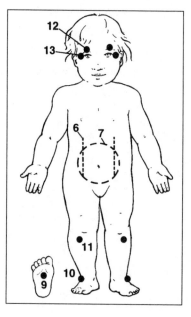

*Refers to main points for brief massage ◆ Numbers on illustrations refer to base plan

VARIATIONS

WITH WIND/COLD ADD:

Press Rotate *Two Leaf Doors* (p. 55)

Press Rotate *Lung Back Point* (p. 66)

Push *Celestial Gate* (p. 73)

Medium: Ginger juice or tea

WITH WIND/HEAT ADD:

Press Rotate *Union Valley* (p. 56)

Push *Six Hollow Bowels* (p. 58)

Press Rotate *Great Hammer* (p. 65)

Medium: Peppermint tea

WITH ABNORMAL DIET ADD:

Push (clear) *Large Intestine Meridian* (p. 51)

Increase repetitions Push *Below Ribs* (p. 61)

Press Rotate to sides of *Spinal Column* (p. 67),
especially *Spleen Back Point* (p. 68), and *Stomach
Back Point* (p. 68)

Medium: Ginger juice

WITH STOMACH HEAT ADD:

Push *Large Transverse Line* (p. 51) to *Wood Gate* (p. 56)

Push *Water of Galaxy* (p. 59)

WITH STOMACH COLD ADD:

Press Rotate *External Palace of Labor* (p. 47)

Increase repetitions Push *Three Passes* (p. 58)

Spinal Pinch Pull *Spinal Column* (p. 67), especially *Spleen Back Point* (p. 68)

Rub Palms Together then cover *Elixir Field* (p. 63)

Medium: Ginger tea

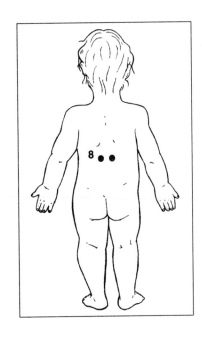

APPENDIX A

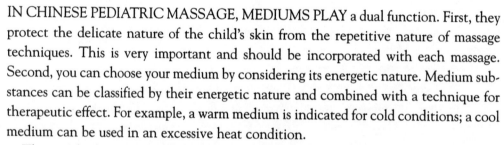

MASSAGE MEDIUMS

IN CHINESE PEDIATRIC MASSAGE, MEDIUMS PLAY a dual function. First, they protect the delicate nature of the child's skin from the repetitive nature of massage techniques. This is very important and should be incorporated with each massage. Second, you can choose your medium by considering its energetic nature. Medium substances can be classified by their energetic nature and combined with a technique for therapeutic effect. For example, a warm medium is indicated for cold conditions; a cool medium can be used in an excessive heat condition.

The standard massage medium for cold or deficient conditions is sesame oil; for hot or excessive conditions, cool or cold water. The massage plans also list some other mediums that you may use instead of the two standards.

Other massage oils, moisturizers, skin cremes, powders, and the like may be used as mediums. Those listed in this appendix are identified for their energetic effect. (Latin names are given for uncommon ingredients.)

Juice Preparations

These mediums are produced by processing the fresh, uncooked materials into a liquid form. Some juices may be extended by adding water.

AGASTACHES (*HERBA AGASTACHES SEU POGOSTEMI*)

Preparation: Pound leaves and stalks, then squeeze.

Properties: Pungent, slightly warm.

Effects: Clear summer heat, resolve damp, rectify qi, harmonize abdomen.

Conditions: Headache, dizziness, nausea, vomiting, chest oppression, itching from insect bites.

CHINESE HAWTHORN *(FRUCTUS CRATAEGI)*

Preparation: Pound and crush.

Properties: Sour, slightly warm.

Effects: Resolves food stagnation.

Conditions: Food stagnation, diarrhea, constipation.

DANDELION

Preparation: Wash, clean, and crush.

Properties: Sweet, bitter, cold.

Effects: Clear heat, detoxify, abate swelling, eliminate stagnation.

Conditions: Lymph gland inflammation, carbuncle, cellulitis, skin infections.

EGG WHITE

Preparation: Separate yolk from white.

Properties: Sweet, salty, placid.

Effects: Strengthen stomach and spleen, moisten skin and lungs, abate swelling, relieve pain, smooth skin, clear pathogenic heat.

Conditions: Toothache, swollen glands, mumps, lymph gland inflammation, sore throat, cough, fever, skin infections, dryness, poxes.

GARLIC

Preparation: Peel, pound, and crush.

Properties: Pungent, warm.

Effects: Detoxify, warm abdomen, invigorate stomach.

Conditions: Common cold, cough, swellings, rashes.

GINGER

Preparation: Pound into pulp, filter juice, and add water.

Properties: Pungent, slightly warm.

Effects: Relieve exterior, disperse cold, warm abdomen, stop vomiting, smooth skin, warm yang qi.

Conditions: Common cold, stiff neck, headache, labored breathing, cough, abdominal pain, diarrhea, vomiting, abdominal distension.

Comments: Used in winter and spring.

LOTUS JUICE

Preparation: Press.

Properties: Sweet, cold.

Effects: Clear heat, promote fluids, cool blood, resolve stagnation.

Conditions: Skin diseases, poxes, infections.

Comments: Use thick and tender roots; slippery and greasy.

LOTUS LEAF

Preparation: Pound and crush.

Properties: Bitter, astringent, placid.

Effects: Clear summer heat, resolve stagnation, stop bleeding.

Conditions: Rubella, pox.

MILK

Preparation: Obtain from a healthy woman, or substitute cow's milk.

Properties: Sweet, salty, placid.

Effects: Tonify deficiency, benefit qi, clear heat, moisten dryness, tonify five organs, support intestinal tract, nourish blood.

Conditions: Conjunctivitis, tic from wind, deficiency gastric disturbance, malnutrition, abdominal pain, diarrhea, urination difficulty, skin pain, itching, chapped or dry skin.

Comments: Use fresh milk.

PEPPERMINT

Preparation: Pound leaves and stalks, then crush.

Properties: Pungent, cool.

Effects: Disperse wind, clear heat, relieve constrained qi, expel pathogenic factors from exterior, smooth skin.

Conditions: External wind or heat, headache, stuffy nose, sore throat, toothache.

Comments: Used in summer.

SCALLION

Preparation: Wash and press.

Properties: Pungent, warm.

Effects: Induce perspiration, promote yang, smooth skin, open meridians, activate circulation, dispel cold.

Conditions: Abdominal pain, urination difficulties.

Comments: Dilute slightly; used in winter and spring.

TRICHOSANTHES FRUIT (*FRUCTUS TRICHOSANTIS*)

Preparation: Peel skin, discard seeds, and crush.

Properties: Sweet, cold.

Effects: Moisten lungs, large intestine, and skin; resolve phlegm, eliminate stagnation.

Conditions: Cough, chest pain, choking.

WATER CHESTNUT

Preparation: Wash, break into pieces, and press.

Properties: Sweet, slightly cold.

Effects: Clear heat, improve eyesight, eliminate stagnation, resolve phlegm.

Conditions: Fever, abdominal mass, jaundice.

Comments: Slippery and greasy.

Water Preparations

Soak herbs in warm or hot water for 20 to 30 minutes or more. Stir occasionally while soaking.

CHRYSANTHEMUM FLOWERS

Preparation: Steep.

Properties: Sweet, bitter, placid.

Effects: Expel wind, clear heat, improve eyesight.

Conditions: Headache, fever, conjunctivitis, eye swelling or pain, dizziness, hypertension.

CINNAMON TWIGS

Preparation: Steep.

Properties: Pungent, sweet, warm.

Effects: Relieve muscles, induce perspiration, warm meridians, tonify yang qi.

Conditions: Common cold with fever, headache, chest oppression, difficult breathing, back pain, frequent urination.

COLD WATER

Properties: Cool.

Effects: Clear heat.

Conditions: Fever.

CORIANDER PLANT (CORIANDRUM SATIVUM)

Preparation: Steep.

Properties: Pungent, slightly warm.

Effects: Induce perspiration, promote eruption, strengthen stomach, facilitate digestion.

Conditions: Measles, poxes.

Comments: Used especially when there is fever but no perspiration.

LOPHATHERUM (HERBA LOPHATHERI GRACILIS)

Preparation: Steep.

Properties: Sweet, cold, placid.

Effects: Clear heat from around heart, eliminate vexation, promote urination, relieve thirst.

Conditions: Restlessness, fever.

MA HUANG (HERBA EPHEDRA)

Preparation: Steep.

Properties: Pungent, slightly bitter, warm.

Effects: Induce perspiration, quell asthma, promote urination.

Conditions: Headache, common cold, asthma, cough, rubella.

MUSK (SECRETIO MOSCHUS MOSCHIFERI)

Preparation: Grind into powder, then steep.

Properties: Pungent, warm.

Effects: Open apertures, activate blood, dissipate stagnation.

Conditions: Coma, epilepsy, unconsciousness, abdominal mass, bruises.

Comments: Expensive.

SCHIZONEPETA AND LEDEBOURIELLAE (HERBA SEU FLOS SCHIZONOPETETA TENUIFOLIAE; RADIX LEDEBOURIELLAE SESLOIDIS)

Preparation: Use 1:1; steep.

Properties: Pungent, warm.

Effects: Relieve exterior, expel wind, resolve damp, alleviate pain.

Conditions: Headache, common cold, throat swelling and pain, joint pain.

SCUTE (*RADIX SCUTELLARIAE BAICALENSIS*)

Preparation: Steep.

Properties: Bitter, cold.

Effects: Clear excess heat, drain damp.

Conditions: Chronic diarrhea, measles, night crying.

Comments: Very strongly heat clearing.

TEA

Preparation: Steep.

Properties: Bitter, sweet, slightly cold.

Effects: Refresh mind, improve eyesight, clear heat, stop thirst, promote digestion, facilitate urination, abate fever.

Conditions: Fever.

Oil Preparations

You can create these mediums by soaking the material in oil, using powdered herbs in oils, or using ointments or other oil-based products.

CARTHAMUS OIL (*FLOS CARTHAMI TINCTORII*)

Preparation: Soak a small amount of carthamus in sesame oil and boil. Use when cool.

Properties: Warm, acrid.

Effects: Moisturizing.

Conditions: Dry skin.

CHINESE ILEX OIL

Properties: Bitter, astringent, neutral.

Effects: Expel wind, tonify deficiency, moisten and nourish skin.

Conditions: Rubella, pain, itching and swelling of skin.

GLYCERIN

Properties: Sweet, neutral.

Effects: Tonify deficiency, moisten dryness.

Conditions: Stomach or spleen deficiency, dry skin.

SESAME OIL

Preparation: Room temperature.

Properties: Sweet, placid, slightly warm.

Effects: Tonify deficiency, strengthen spleen, moisten dryness.

Conditions: Malnutrition, stomach or spleen deficiency, dry and rough skin.

Comments: Standard massage medium.

APPENDIX B

EXTERNAL CHINESE HERBAL REMEDIES

THE USE OF EXTERNAL APPLICATIONS OF HERBS in pediatrics has a long history and is common among Chinese parents for home treatment of simple conditions. Unfortunately, there is little written material on this subject. Here are several applications and their actions.

Abdominal Distension, Food Retention

MIRABILITUM OR RHUBARB
(MIRABILITUM DEPURATUM; RHIZOMA RHEI)

Preparation: Crush.

Properties: Bitter, cold.

Effects: Clear obstructions, drain heat.

Comments: Wrap herbs in a packet, place on the navel, and secure with a sash around the waist. Monitor for skin irritation.

Chronic Diarrhea

CLOVE AND CINNAMON BARK

Preparation: Powder.

Properties: Acrid, warm.

Effects: Warm abdomen and kidneys.

Comments: Apply to the navel.

GARLIC

Preparation: Crush.

Properties: Acrid, warm.

Effects: Remove toxins.

Comments: Wrap in a packet and tie to the navel or the sole of the foot.

Colic, Food Accumulation, Internal Cold

SCALLION STALK, GINGER, AND WHEAT BRAN

Preparation: Heat briefly.

Properties: Pungent, warm.

Effects: Dispel cold, warm abdomen.

Comments: Wrap in a packet while warm, apply to the navel, and secure with a sash around the waist.

Measles

CORIANDER (CORIANDRUM SATIVUM)

Preparation: Steam.

Properties: Pungent, slightly warm.

Effects: Promote eruption of measles.

Comments: Apply to painful or itching, unerupted locations. A tea may be used as a massage medium for measles.

Mumps

PURSLANE (HERBA PORTULACEA OLERACEAE)

Preparation: Pound.

Properties: Sour, cold.

Effects: Relieve swelling, clear heat.

Comments: Use fresh herbs; apply to the swollen area of the neck.

HIBISCUS (*FOLUIM HIBISCUS MUTABILIS*)

Preparation: Pound.

Properties: Pungent, neutral.

Effects: Cool blood, remove toxins, disperse swelling, control pain.

Comments: Use fresh herbs; apply to neck area.

VEGETABLE SPONGE (*FASCICULUS VASCULARIS LUFFAE*)

Preparation: Pound.

Properties: Sweet, neutral.

Effects: Expel wind.

Comments: Use fresh herbs; apply to the neck area.

Night Sweats

CHINESE GALL (*GALLA RHI CHINESIS*)

Preparation: Powder.

Properties: Sour, salty, cold.

Effects: Retain fluids.

Comments: Mix with vinegar into a paste and place on the navel before sleep.

Pneumonia

RANUNCULUS (*RADIX RANUCULI TERNATI*)

Preparation: Pound with sugar.

Properties: Sweet, pungent, warm.

Effects: Disperse heat and swelling.

Comments: Use fresh herbs; apply to the focus area of the chest.

Urination Difficulties

FRESH SCALLION

Preparation: Mix with salt.

Properties: Pungent, warm.

Effects: Dispel cold.

Comments: Apply on the navel and lower abdomen.

APPENDIX C

RECOMMENDED RESOURCES

Chinese Medicine Principles

For a general introduction to concepts and principles of Chinese medicine:

Beinfield, Harriet, and Efrem Korngold. *Between Heaven and Earth*. New York: Ballantine Books, 1991.

Kaptchuk, Ted. *The Web That Has No Weaver*. New York: Congdon and Weed, Inc., 1983.

For more detailed information suitable for practitioners:

Maciocia, Giovanni. *The Foundations of Chinese Medicine*. New York: Churchill Livingston, 1989.

Wiseman, Nigel. *Fundamentals of Chinese Medicine*. Brookline, Mass.: Paradigm Publications, 1985.

Chinese Pediatric Massage

Videos that demonstrate techniques and show a pediatric massage:

Cline, Kyle. *A Parent's Guide to Chinese Pediatric Massage Reference Video*. Portland, Oreg.: Institute for Traditional Medicine, 1994. (A good companion to this book.)

————. *Chinese Pediatric Massage—Practitioner's Reference Video*. Portland, Oreg.: Institute for Traditional Medicine, 1993.

————. *Introduction to Chinese Pediatric Massage*. Portland, Oreg.: Institute for Traditional Medicine, 1993. (A 30-minute introduction, including demonstrations and interviews with parents who use the massage.)

————. *Colic Relief: A Chinese Pediatric Massage Approach*. Portland, Oreg.: Institute for Traditional Medicine, 1996.

Other Books on Chinese Pediatric Massage

Cline, Kyle. *Chinese Pediatric Massage—A Practitioner's Guide*. Rochester, Vermont: Healing Arts Press, 1999. (Intended for practitioners of Oriental medicine.)

————. *Colic Relief: A Chinese Pediatric Massage Approach*. Portland, Oreg.: Institute for Traditional Medicine, 1996.

Chinese Medicine and Pediatrics

Flaws, Bob. *Food, Phlegm & Pediatric Diseases* (pamphlet). Boulder, Colo.: Blue Poppy Press. (Information on diet and children.)

————. *Keeping Your Child Healthy with Chinese Medicine: A Parent's Guide to the Care & Prevention of Common Childhood Diseases*. Boulder, Colo.: Blue Poppy Press, 1996.

————. *A Handbook of TCM Pediatrics*. Boulder, Colo.: Blue Poppy Press, 1977. (Written for Oriental medicine practitioners.)

Wolfe, Honora. *How to Have a Healthy Pregnancy, Healthy Birth*. Boulder, Colo.: Blue Poppy Press, 1993.

The Institute for Traditional Medicine may be reached at 1-800-544-7504. Blue Poppy Press may be reached at 1-800-487-9296.

GLOSSARY OF CHINESE ENERGETIC TERMINOLOGY

THE TERMINOLOGY OF TRADITIONAL CHINESE MEDICINE varies from book to book, depending on the author and translation style. The following words and concepts used within this book are briefly defined here for clarity.

Blood

Blood is yin in relation to qi (yang). A very dense substance providing nourishment, moistening, and a material foundation for the body.

Clear

The energetic intent of a treatment technique (such as, to clear the lung meridian of accumulated heat by using the Push technique). Opposite of tonify. Synonyms: reduce, expel.

Cold

One aspect of the Eight Principles. Cold is an energetic quality manifesting in the body. Common attributes of cold include cold sensations in the body, desire for warmth, contraction, and obstruction.

Congenital qi

One type of qi in the body. Congenital qi is the combination of qi inherited from both parents at conception. This is the foundation from which development and constitution derive. Synonyms: heredity qi, preheaven essence, prenatal qi, congenital essence.

Damp

One aspect of the six pathogenic factors. Dampness is a yin pathogenic factor and refers to the damp quality of weather or to living or working environment. Damp is characterized by heaviness, stickiness, and slowed movement.

Defensive qi

One type of qi in the body. Defensive qi is responsible for the outer defense of the body. It prevents external pathogenic factors from invading the body. Synonym: protective qi. (Pinyin: wei qi.)

Deficiency

One aspect of the Eight Principles. Deficiency is yin relative to excess (yang). Deficiency describes an energetic condition that is weak or has too little, less than enough (such as, deficiency in the lung meridian). Synonyms: vacuity, emptiness, insufficiency.

Dietary therapy

One of the therapeutic modalities of traditional Chinese medicine. Dietary therapy is the use of daily foods to bring about an energetic result. Dietary therapy can play a very significant role in the overall treatment plan because it is such an integral aspect of daily living.

Essence

A very refined, primary substance. Essence describes the cumulative congenital and postnatal energies, which are the basis of growth, development, quality of life, and length of life. Essence is a primary foundation substance that supports the rest of the body's energetic functions.

Excess

One aspect of the Eight Principles. Excess is yang in relation to deficiency (yin). Excess describes an energetic condition that is overfull, or too much (such as, excess heat of the lung meridian). Synonyms: replete, overfull.

Exterior

One aspect of the Eight Principles. Exterior is yang in relation to interior (yin).

Exterior refers to the outer and surface parts of the body: skin, body hair, muscles, superficial meridians.

External pathogenic invasion

Describes the process of one or more pathogenic factors (wind, cold, dry, damp, fire, summer heat) penetrating the body's outer defenses. The quality of the combined pathogenic factors then influences the person's energetic pattern. Synonyms: six pernicious influences, six external evils.

Fluids

Include all of the normal liquid substances of the body: sweat, saliva, urine, and so on. The main functions of fluids are to moisten, lubricate, and nourish.

Heat

One aspect of the Eight Principles. Heat is yang in relation to cold (yin). Heat is an energetic quality manifesting in the body. Heat indicators include hot sensations in the body, elevated temperature, desire for coolness, burning pain.

Herbal therapy

The use of substances from the plant, animal, and mineral kingdoms to influence the energetic nature of the body. Application of herbal therapy can be internal or external.

Interior

One aspect of the Eight Principles. Interior is yin in relation to exterior (yang). Interior describes the internal aspects of the body: organs, bone, internal meridians.

Meridians

The pathways that transport qi, blood, and fluids throughout the body. Meridians function to connect all aspects of the body and maintain communication, forming an integrated whole. Synonyms: vessels, channels.

Pathogenic

Descriptive of a certain level or amount of energy (cold, damp, heat, etc.) that is capable of producing imbalance, disharmony, or disease.

Pattern of disharmony

Describes the energetic nature of an imbalance, illness, or disease. Pattern of disharmony refers to the relationship between energetic aspects in the body (such as, excessive liver yang).

Qi

A difficult word to translate into English (which is why *qi* is used instead of a translation). Qi is a very subtle vibration, or energy, that has not quite manifested into a material form. This is why qi has not been physically seen or measured. However, the effects and results of qi can be easily understood on a physical level. For example, applying finger pressure to a point will generally result in both practitioner and patient experiencing some sensations of qi (tingling, warmth, movement, etc.). Synonyms: chi, ch'i, energy, ether, prana, breath, lifeforce, vital force.

Shen

The external manifestation of the internal essence. Shen describes the overall physical, mental, and spiritual vitality of a person's energetic nature. Synonyms: spirit, mind, consciousness.

Stagnation

Describes a sluggishness of movement. Stagnation may involve qi, blood, fluids, or materials through the body. Synonym: stasis.

Tonify

A method of correcting an energetic deficiency. Tonify refers to a treatment or technique that replenishes an energetic level that is lacking (e.g., tonify deficient lung yin). Synonyms: supplement, reinforce, nourish, fortify.

Traditional Chinese medicine (TCM)

The reorganization of Chinese medicine by the People's Republic of China government after the Communist Revolution in 1949. The development of TCM brought together many disparate segments of Chinese medicine into a unified system. TCM is the standard Oriental medical system used in the People's Republic of China and the predominant Oriental system in the United States.

Tui na

One of the three main branches of traditional Chinese medicine. Tui na is the use of hand manipulations to influence energetic conditions in the body. Synonyms: massotherapy, Chinese medical massage.

Wind

One of the six external pathogens. Wind refers to the energetic qualities of swiftness, movement, rapid onset, and changeable nature.

Yang

Describes phenomena that are relatively more energetic. Yang corresponds to creation, activity, ascension, expansion, immateriality, heat, fire, summer, and so on.

Yin

Describes phenomena that are relatively more material. Yin corresponds to matter, structure, form, substance, contraction, descent, cold, water, winter, and so on.

Yin-yang

A theory used throughout Oriental philosophy and medicine. Yin-yang theory describes all phenomena in the universe as pairs of complementary opposites. Still, although they are opposites, together yin and yang form a complementary whole and are interdependent. Nothing is totally yin or totally yang.

BIBLIOGRAPHY

Primary Sources

English Language

Cao Ji-ming, et al., eds. *Essentials of Traditional Chinese Pediatrics*. Beijing: Foreign Languages Press, 1990.

Cline, Kyle. *Chinese Pediatric Massage: A Practitioner's Guide*. Rochester, Vermont: Healing Arts Press, 1999.

Fan Yi-li. *Chinese Pediatric Massage Therapy*. Boulder, Colo.: Blue Poppy Press, 1994.

Flaws, Bob. *Turtle Tails and Other Tender Mercies: Traditional Chinese Pediatrics*. Boulder, Colo.: Blue Poppy Press, 1985.

Luan Chang-ye. *Infantile Tuina Therapy*. Beijing: Foreign Languages Press, 1989.

Sun Cheng-nan, ed. *Chinese Massage Therapy*. Jinan, China: Shandong Science and Technology Press, 1990.

Tiquia, Rey. *Chinese Infant Massage*. Richmond, Victoria, Australia: Greenhouse Publications, Ltd., 1986.

Xiao Shu-qin. *Pediatric Bronchitis: Its TCM Cause, Diagnosis, Treatment and Prevention*. Boulder, Colo.: Blue Poppy Press, 1991.

Zhang En-qin, ed. *Chinese Massage*. Shanghai: Publishing House of Shanghai College of Traditional Chinese Medicine, 1990.

Secondary Sources

Beinfield, Harriet and Efrem Korngold. *Between Heaven and Earth: A Guide to Chinese Medicine*. New York: Ballantine Books, 1991.

Bensky, Dan. *Chinese Herbal Medicine Materia Medica*. Seattle: Eastland Press, 1986.

———. *Chinese Herbal Medicine: Formulas and Strategies*. Seattle: Eastland Press, 1990.

Cao Guo-liang. *Essentials of Tuinaology: Chinese Medical Massage and Manipulation*. Hilo, Hawaii: Cao's Fire Dragon, 1988.

Chen Ze-lin and Chen Mei-fang. *A Comprehensive Guide to Chinese Herbal Medicine*. Long Beach, Calif.: Oriental Healing Arts Institute, 1992.

Cheng Xin-nong, ed. *Chinese Acupuncture and Moxibustion*. Bejing: Foreign Languages Press, 1987.

Cui Yue-li. *The Chinese-English Medical Dictionary*. Beijing: People's Medical Publishing House, 1987.

Dharmananda, Subhuti. *Chinese Herbology*. Portland, Oreg.: Institute for Traditional Medicine, 1990.

Ellis, Andrew. *Grasping the Wind*. Brookline, Mass.: Paradigm Publications, 1989.

Flaws, Bob. *A Handbook of TCM Pediatrics*. Boulder, Colo.: Blue Poppy Press, 1997.

Fratkin, Jake. *Chinese Herbal Patent Formulas*. Santa Fe: SHYA Publications, 1986.

Hsu Hong-yen. *Commonly Used Chinese Herb Formulas with Illustrations*. Long Beach, Calif.: Oriental Healing Arts Institute Press, 1990.

———. *Commonly Used Chinese Herbal Formulas: Companion Handbook*. Long Beach, Calif.: Oriental Healing Arts Institute Press, 1997.

———. *Oriental Materia Medica: A Concise Guide*. Long Beach, Calif.: Oriental Healing Arts Institute Press, 1986.

Kaptchuk, Ted. *The Web That Has No Weaver*. New York: Congdon and Weed, Inc., 1983.

Lade, A. *Chinese Massage: A Handbook of Therapeutic Massage*. Vancouver, B.C., Canada: Hartley and Marks, 1987.

Maciocia, Giovanni. *The Foundations of Chinese Medicine*. New York: Churchill Livingston, 1989.

Naeser, Margaret. *Outline Guide to Chinese Herbal Patent Medicines in Pill Form*. Boston: Boston Chinese Medicine, 1993.

Sun Shu-chun. *Atlas of Therapeutic Motion for Treatment and Health*. Beijing: Foreign Languages Press, 1989.

Taber, Clarence. *Taber's Cyclopedic Medical Dictionary*. Philadelphia: F. A. Davis Company, 1989.

Unschuld, Paul. *Medicine in China: A History of Ideas*. Berkeley: University of

California Press, 1985.

Wiseman, Nigel. *Fundamentals of Chinese Medicine*. Brookline, Mass.: Paradigm Publications, 1985.

Wu Jing-ying. *A Chinese-English Dictionary*. Beijing: Commercial Business Printing Company, 1989.

Xie Zhu-fan. *Dictionary of Traditional Chinese Medicine*. Hong Kong: The Commercial Press, Ltd., 1984.

Yeung Him-che. *Handbook of Chinese Herbs and Formulas*. Los Angeles: Institute of Chinese Medicine, 1985.

Zhu Chun-han. *Clinical Handbook of Prepared Chinese Medicines*. Brookline, Mass.: Paradigm Publications, 1989.

INDEX

Massage Plans

Points

Techniques